DRINK, DRUGS AND GAMBLING

DRINK, DRUGS
AND
GAMBLING

M. K. GANDHI

EDITED BY

BHARATAN KUMARAPPA

GYAN

Published by

Gyan Publishing House
5, Ansari Road
Daryaganj, New Delhi-110002
Phone: 011-47034999, 9811692060
E-mail: books@gyanbooks.com

Distribution Network
gyanbooks.com
India, USA, Canada, UK, Australia

ISBN: 978-93-6920-514-1 (HB)

First Published, 1952

2nd Impression 2025

Printed at: Gyan Press, Delhi.

DRINK, DRUGS AND GAMBLING
Author: M. K. GANDHI, Edited by BHARATAN KUMARAPPA

DRINK, DRUGS AND GAMBLING

By

M. K. GANDHI

NAVAJIVAN PUBLISHING HOUSE
AHMEDABAD-14

DRINK, DRUGS AND GAMBLING

By
M. K. GANDHI

Edited by
BHARATAN KUMARAPPA

NAVAJIVAN PUBLISHING HOUSE
AHMEDABAD-14

EDITOR'S NOTE

Gandhiji, with his shrewd insight into all matters relating to non-violence, recognized that non-violent conduct, whether in the individual or social sphere, presupposed strength of character and self-control.

Nor was this in any way original to him. It was the teaching of the *Gita* which he recited morning and evening in his daily prayers, and which taught that the 'illumined' man will draw away from sense-objects even as a tortoise draws inward its limbs. He will control his senses, for attachment to sense-objects leads to passion, anger, mental confusion and thus to mental instability and chaos. Under the influence of his lust, man loses balance, sees things in an exaggerated form and indulges in conduct which he later regrets, and which brings unhappiness to himself and to those around him. Lust involves him at times in abuse, brawls, cruelty to his family and others, physical violence, and even murder. Our fathers therefore taught that the greatest enemy of happiness and peace was sensual attachment or passion, that man must be weaned from being a mere animal, from being a slave of blind momentary impulse; or stated positively, that he must be taught to strengthen his will and learn to guide himself by the universal laws of Reason.

Consequently, although drink was originally very popular with our people, it was soon banished out of decent society. It was a great achievement that intoxicating drink which was once offered to the gods, was later deprived of all respectability and condemned to exist only among those who were considered to constitute the lowest stratum of society. Even tappers of toddy, though they may not themselves drink, are up to this day regarded in some parts of our country as 'untouchables' evidently only because they are associated with the liquor trade.

As against centuries of such teaching and tradition in our country, what did Gandhiji find but that under the influence and encouragement of an alien Government which derived a large revenue from excise, drink, drugs and gambling, which tended to enslave man, were gaining ground and steadily spreading throughout the land. He was convinced that these were even more to be resisted than foreign rule, for if unarrested they were bound to eat into the very vitals of the nation, and make it weak and degenerate.

Nor was he alone in his opposition to drink. Temperance societies run by Indians and others existed. They carried on propaganda against drink, and requested the Government to make liquor more expensive by levying higher taxes on intoxicating drinks and to reduce the number of liquor shops and their hours of business. But Gandhiji found that even half a century of such work had proved ineffective to prevent the evil from spreading.

Besides, when he went to England he saw his fellow-barristers rolling in the gutters under the influence of liquor. He never got over the shock. He saw with horror drink spreading also amongst his own countrymen in South Africa, and when he returned to India and observed that the Government was raising revenue by licensing liquor shops and dealers, he determined to put an end to such Governmental sanction of vice.

Under his leadership the Indian National Congress included prohibition of liquor and opium as part of the Non-Co-operation Movement of 1920-22. Gandhiji made use of the network of Congress organization throughout the country to carry on his crusade against drink and drugs and to urge prohibition of these on the Government. Congressmen and women rallied to his support, hindered auctioning of licences to liquor dealers, and picketed liquor shops. As the result of such country-wide campaign many persons gave up drink, and liquor revenue fell rapidly, much to the discomfiture of the Government.

It was not as though Gandhiji sought through prohibition to bring about moral reform. He realized that such reform must come from within and cannot be enforced by law. What he hoped to achieve by prohibition, therefore, was not to prevent people from drinking but to prevent the sale of liquor and drugs, so as to remove temptation from the way of the addict. As he repeatedly says, helpless victims of drink want to be helped against themselves. They know the evil effect of drink on themselves, and the misery and poverty it brings to their families, and yet they cannot pass by an open liquor shop without going in and indulging themselves. So he insisted that the Government should close down liquor shops and prohibit the sale of liquor. It is true that when faced with closed liquor shops, some drunkards may produce liquor surreptitiously or find worse substitutes. But such people, he believed, will be comparatively few, and places which deal in such drinks can be dealt with by law.

Accordingly when the Congress came into power in 1937 and formed cabinets, it introduced prohibition of liquor in parts of Madras, Bombay, U. P., Bihar, C. P. and the North West Frontier Province. It prohibited opium in Assam and Orissa — the Provinces of India where indulgence in this drug was most prevalent. Its intention was to launch out on prohibition in selected areas and then spread out gradually to cover the whole country. In this way, it was thought that difficulties such as loss of revenue and expenditure on preventive and propaganda staff could be met.

In addition to such legal ban on drink and drugs, the Congress Governments obtained the help of private institutions to carry on educational propaganda among all classes. Counter-attractions such as recreation centres for music, drama, etc. were provided, and in industrial areas shops were opened where aerated waters, milk and butter-milk could be bought at cost price. It was also sought to find employment for those who were thrown out of work owing to prohibition.

The Congress cabinets resigned, however, in 1939 owing to the British Government in India plunging the country in the second World War without so much as consulting the legislatures. With their resignation, the British Government of India scrapped prohibition and went back once more to raising revenue from liquor licences.

With the dawn of freedom, however, in 1947, the Congress has again launched on a policy of prohibition of liquor throughout the country in gradual stages. In regard to drugs, Assam and Orissa have prohibited the sale of opium for smoking and eating, and the conference of Ministers of Excise which met at New Delhi in August 1949 resolved to achieve complete prohibition of opium for such purposes throughout the country within the next ten years. And in respect of gambling, the Bombay Government has decided to put an end to horse-racing very shortly.

Dr. H. C. Mukerjee, Calcutta, had collected the matter contained in this volume, but was unfortunately unable to complete the work of editing it, owing to ill-health and lack of time.

In this collection are included Gandhiji's writings (often only in extract form), and reports of his talks on drink, drugs, smoking and gambling. He himself said that for him intoxicants meant all these habit-forming indulgences, even tea.

Under Drink and Drugs we have given in Part II of each of these topics selections from the writings of others, which Gandhiji published in his paper, as supplementing what he had to say. In a book which purports to be by Gandhiji we could, of course, include only as few of such writings as possible.

Prohibition is still meeting with opposition from interested parties, and a few others who object to it chiefly because in their opinion the Government cannot afford to forgo the revenue from liquor at this time. In the great task which our Free Government has undertaken in this regard it is certain that Gandhiji's earnest pleadings against intoxicants and enslaving habits will prove most valuable. Let us hope that our country, now freed from alien domination, will live up to its ancient heritage, and show the way for man to achieve self-mastery and sane rational living without which non-violence and peace must remain an empty dream.

Bombay, October 1951 BHARATAN KUMARAPPA

NON-ENGLISH WORDS WITH THEIR MEANINGS

Abkari — excise
Ahimsa — non-violence
Arrack — liquor drawn from the palm trees; also spirit made from rice or molasses
Ashram — a place of retirement; Gandhiji's colony run on a spiritual basis
Bania — a member of the trader caste; one given to thinking only of profit and loss
Bhajan — prayer in the form of a song
Bidi — country cigarette
Charkha — spinning wheel
Daru — intoxicating drink
Ganja — flower of Indian hemp which has an intoxicating effect when smoked with tobacco
Gur — jaggery; unrefined brown product derived from palm juice or sugarcane juice, and used as sugar
Harijan — literally, people of God; a name given to 'untouchables' by Gandhiji
Khadi, Khaddar — hand-spun, hand-woven cloth
Lakh — 1,00,000
Mahura — a flower from which liquor is extracted
Munsiff — village judge
Nira — sweet, unfermented juice of the palm tree
Paddy — unhusked rice
Pandal — a temporary roof made of cloth, leaves or mats
Sardar — chieftain; a title, often used for Sikhs as a term of respect or courtesy
Seer — a weight a little over 2 lbs.
Swaraj — self-government
Taj — Taj Mahal Hotel, a large hotel in Bombay
Takli — spindle used in spinning without a wheel
Tamasha — fun and amusement; entertainment
Toddy — juice derived from the palm tree; liquor from the same source
Tola — unit of weight = 180 grains troy; 2½ tolas = 1 ounce

CONTENTS

D. JEWS

E. PARSIS

DRINK

PART II : By Others

DRUGS

PART I : By Gandhiji

DRUGS

PART II : By Others

TEA, COFFEE AND TOBACCO

By Gandhiji

GAMBLING

By Gandhiji

DRINK, DRUGS AND GAMBLING

DRINK

PART I: *By Gandhiji*

I. DRINK IN RELATION TO GOVERNMENTS

A. UNDER BRITISH GOVERNMENT

1. IN BRITISH INDIA

1

TO THE MODERATES

I ask you to accept my evidence, that the country as a whole is sick of the drink curse. Those unfortunate men who have become slaves to the habit, require to be helped against themselves. Some of them even ask to be helped. I invite you to take advantage of the wave of feeling that has been roused against the drink traffic. The agitation arose spontaneously. Believe me, the deprivation to the Government of the drink revenue is of the least importance in the campaign. The country is simply impatient of the evil itself. In no country in the world, will it be possible to carry on this traffic in the face of the united and the enlightened opposition of a people such as is now to be witnessed in India. Whatever the errors or excesses that were committed by the mob in Nagpur, the cause was just. The people were determined to do away with the drink curse that was sapping their vitality. You will not be deceived by the specious argument that India must not be made sober by compulsion and that those who wish to drink must have facilities provided for them. The State does not cater for the vices of its people. We do not regulate or license houses of ill fame. We do not provide facilities for thieves to indulge their propensity for thieving. I hold drink to be more damnable than thieving and perhaps even prostitution. Is it not often the parent of both? I ask you to join the country in sweeping out of existence the drink revenue and abolishing the liquor-shops.

***Young India*, 8-6-'21**

2

EXCISE AND EDUCATION

It is no matter of pride to us that our children are being educated out of the revenue derived from this immoral source. I would almost forgive the Council entry by Congressmen, if they would boldly sweep out this revenue even though education may have to be starved. Nothing of the kind should happen if they will insist on a corresponding reduction in the military expenditure.

Young India, 26-12-'24

3

TERMS. OF PROHIBITION

The Governor of Bombay has plainly told the Anjuman of Broach that if they want prohibition they must find fresh sources of revenue to replace the revenue derived from drink. In other words it is no concern of the Government to arrest the evil of drink. It is the duty of the reformer to supply the revenue lost by return to sobriety. Prohibitionists therefore, if they want early prohibition, will have to make up their minds as to their reply to H. E. the Governor of Bombay which represents in this case the policy of the Government of India.

Young India, 11-2-'26

4

VIOLENCE IN DHARWAD

If the Congress Committee's telegram to the *Chronicle* may be relied upon, there is little doubt that some unauthorized police officer has been panic-stricken and given the order to fire on an unarmed crowd. The persistent keeping open of liquor-shops as if it was a right of the public to have liquor served to it by the State, is an open and immoral defiance of public opinion. I can only congratulate the families of those who have died. I can deplore the slightest show of force that may have been betrayed by the crowd, but I respectfully warn the Indian Ministers in charge of transferred departments, that they will belie the traditions of the great party to which they belong, if they do not courageously face the grave crisis that is overtaking the country, and summarily close every liquor-shop and refund the money paid in advance by the poor licence-holders. They may not dread the loss of revenue immorally derived from the twice cursed traffic. It cannot stand in the face of an awakened and enraged public conscience. As it is, an education supported by a revenue derived from an immoral source is bad enough. Presently, it will stink in our nostrils when it is tainted with innocent blood. I do beseech the Ministers to be warned before it is too late. Let it not be said of them that for the sake of revenue they remained callously indifferent to the signs of the times. They dare not wait for hours, much less for weeks. It will be wrong to wait for devising methods of tapping other sources of revenue before giving up the revenue from drink. It will be very like a man refusing to vacate a plague-infected house until another is ready for him. Most people in such circumstances will first vacate, and then search for another and uninfected shelter.

Young India, 6-7-'21

5

VIRTUE PENALIZED

> "The renter's explanation for not working the shop and for not tapping and drawing toddy from the trees for the shop is unsatisfactory. He is fined Rs. 50."

Such is the entry in the proceedings of the Revenue Divisional Officer of Namakal in the Madras Presidency. The reader knows that the shop is a drink shop. The renter's explanation was that the drinkers had decided not to drink and therefore he saw no use in keeping the shop open. He was however willing to pay the rent. This explanation was not satisfactory. Nor was it enough that the abstaining villagers were ready to pay the Government the whole year's stipulated profits from the drink traffic for the luxury of indulging in their newly acquired virtue of abstinence. That was not to be, for the law was against them. If the whole of the proceedings were legally examined, it will probably be found that the officials concerned could give no other decision. They are not at fault. It is the system that is bad, for in that system revenue is the primary consideration, not the health of the soul or the body. Had it been otherwise, the drink and the opium traffic would have gone long ago. I do hope that the villagers and the poor renter will have the strength to withstand all fines and other penalties for the reform they have inaugurated.

Young India, 22-5-'24

6

PROHIBITION

Sjt. C. Rajagopalachari who has been entrusted with the prohibition propaganda by the Working Committee has issued the first number of the monthly *Prohibition*, the official organ of the Prohibition League of India. Its price is 2 annas, postage extra, and can be had at Gandhi Ashram, Tiruchengodu. The contents are interesting. They show how the Government thwart prohibition by every means at their disposal. Damoh is a district of the Central Provinces. It carried prohibition in the teeth of opposition. I must ask the curious to read the history of the campaign in the pages of the journal. I cannot however resist quoting the following tragic story of damages claimed by a liquor vendor:

> "Perumal Naidu, Village Munsiff of Singarapet, District Salem, Madras, was tried departmentally by the Divisional Revenue Officer on the following charges:
>
> (1) That he proclaimed by beat of drum that none in the village should drink toddy; (2) that he took pledges from Adi-Dravidas not to drink; (3) that he organized caste discipline against drink and levied fines from those who broke the rule; and (4) that he beat one Nollayan for having got drunk.
>
> "Perumal Naidu did not admit the charges but pleaded that he always assisted Government. In his own picturesque language, 'It was his end and aim and bounden duty to support the Government and render all assistance

to it to realize good income in such matters, and that he had been doing so and never went amiss.'

"The man's plea was however not believed and he was suspended for one year by the Divisional Officer. Said this officer in the concluding para of his order, which is the only para of which copy was given, the rest being 'confidential':

'In conclusion, I hold that it has been proved beyond any doubt that there was a campaign against drink in the village and that it was tom-tommed in the village that nobody should drink toddy: that the village munsiff failed in his duty in not having reported it to the authorities. There are strong reasons to suggest that he connived at this campaign, if he did not actively participate in it. His antecedents show that he is apt to do very high-handed actions. Still in consideration of his 25 years' service I give him a chance to improve. I suspend him for one year from the date on which he was relieved with severe warning that if he gives room to any complaint hereafter he will be dismissed from service.' (D. No. 3469 of 26 — 5th April 1927).

"Not content with the infliction of this departmental punishment the local toddy shop renter filed a suit for damages for Rs 300/- on the ground that by reason of the defendant's dissuasion, he lost all custom for full three months, January to March 1926, and that the defendant was bound to make good the loss. The Munsiff framed the following issues:

(1) Whether the suit should not have been brought within one year from the date of accrual of cause of action; (2) Whether the defendant did the acts attributed to him and caused any loss to the plaintiff of which the law should take notice; (3) If so, to what extent is the defendant bound to make good that loss.

"The suit is pending."

Is it any wonder if I call a system satanic under which such things are possible? I need not be told that there may be other systems more satanic than this. It would be time enough to consider such a retort if I had to make a choice between satanic systems. The pity of it is that many educated Indians who lead public opinion are drawn into this satanic net as witness what Mahadev Desai said about the recent dinner to the Viceroy at the Chelmsford Club. All but one or two Indians drank champagne to their fill! When Satan comes disguised as a champion of liberty, civilization, culture and the like, he makes himself almost irresistible.

It is therefore a good thing that prohibition is an integral part of the Congress programme.

Young India, 11-7-'29

7

PROHIBITION AND MADRAS GOVERNMENT

Sjt. C. Rajagopalachari has unearthed a Government order which is simplicity itself but which conveys a world of meaning. In a note accompanying a copy of the order Sjt. Rajagopalachari writes to the Press:

> "Among the many post-Reform additions to our recurring charges are the new Health Officers and their staff. They are expected to educate the people about cholera, malaria, etc."

Some of the members of the staff seem to have enquired whether they should carry on propaganda against the drink habit also and the laconic reply received was:

> "The Government consider that the Public Health Staff should not carry on anti-drink propaganda."

It is to be noted here that there is no reason assigned for the ban on anti-drink propaganda. On the contrary, one would expect explicit instructions to these conservators of health to instruct the people about the evil effects of drink on the body under a popular Government. They would be required to tell the people how deadly the effect of alcohol is upon the human body and show by magic lantern slides in a graphic manner the ruin that alcohol brings wherever it finds a place. But it is madness to expect the existing Government to do any such thing. One may as well expect the keeper of a public house to warn its visitors against running into the death-trap. Is not the Government the keeper of all the public houses of India? It is the 25 crores revenue that enables us to give University education to our children. It enables the Government to impose *pax Britannica* upon us. Not till the people realize their duty and develop strength to resist the Government in its pro-drink policy, will it be possible to have a dry India.

Young India, 6-5-'26

TOTAL PROHIBITION

The Swaraj Party in Madras deserves the congratulations of all friends of the poor for having included total prohibition in their programme. Were it not for the very potential force of inertia we would long since have done away with this evil. It is sapping the vitality of the labouring classes, who need to be helped against themselves. There is no country in the world which is so well-fitted for immediate prohibition as India. Public opinion has always been on the right path. No referendum is necessary as it would be in European countries, for the simple reason that in India the intellectual classes do not drink as in European countries. The Rev. W. L. Ferguson of Madras has brought out a pamphlet clearly showing the need for prohibition. Of the financial burden the reverend gentleman says:

> " No country, however rich and prosperous, can really afford to drink, for drink brings nations to the verge of ruin and sometimes topples them over the brink. India is a poor country as yet. She is poor in her capital wealth; she is poor in education; she is poor in sanitation and public health; she is poor in housing; she is poor in agriculture and manufacturing; she is poor in means of communication in rural areas; and if there is any department of her life in which she does not need more of good than she possesses, let some knowing one inform us, for we do not know what or where it is. India cannot afford the use of intoxicants. Financially the drain is too heavy. Just what the cost is in rupees we are unable to say; but some idea of it can be obtained from the revenues derived by the Government in the Excise Department. In round numbers this is Rs 20,00,00,000 per annum. Some estimate that the total drink and drug bill of India for a year amounts to five times this sum received by Government; and others place it at three times that figure. I do not believe that we shall err very far if we take a figure half way between these two and place the amount at Rs. 80,00,00,000. Now of this vast sum the greater part comes from the earnings of the labouring classes, — the very people who need it most for promoting the welfare of themselves, their families and their communities. If we assume that three-fourths of the drink and drug bill of India is paid by the poor and the labouring classes, some Rs 60,00,00,000 is the burden they are bearing. And what could be done towards putting India's poor on their feet, if this vast revenue annually

were saved from intoxicants and used for home-building and nation-building enterprises! It would not be long before thrift would replace squalor in our great cities and prosperity begins to attend the humble dwellings of our villages."

The moral loss is even greater than the financial. Drinks and drugs degrade those who are addicted to them and those who traffic in them. The drunkard forgets the distinction between wife, mother and sister and indulges in crimes of which in his sober moments he will be ashamed. Any one who has anything to do with labour knows to what state the labourers are reduced when they are under the satanic influence of drink. Nor are the other classes better off. I have known the captain of a ship forgetting himself in his drunken state. The ship had to be entrusted to the care of the chief officer. Barristers having drunk have been known to be rolling in gutters. Only these better-placed men are protected by the police all over the world whereas the poor drunkard is punished for his poverty.

Young India, 4-2-'26

9

DOES INDIA WANT PROHIBITION?

Much has been made by the opponents of total prohibition in India on the speech of Mr King, Financial Commissioner in the Punjab, who was reported to have said that the Local Option Act which was passed over a year ago in the Punjab has been a perfect failure. The Commissioner quotes in support of his statement the following facts:

That out of nearly 200 Municipalities, District Boards etc., only 19 have asked to be empowered under the Act. Of the 19, only 6 took further steps. And in the 6 the *referendum* that was held had precious little support. At Rawalpindi for instance out of 7,000 voters, only six registered their votes. At Ludhiana out of 12,500 voters at the first *referendum* not one turned up. A second date was fixed at which only four turned up. Of other four only in one small town, that of Tohana, out of 1,052 voters, 802 voted for total prohibition.

Mr King argued, as he would be entitled to argue if he

was a stranger to India and Indian conditions, that there was no demand for total prohibition in the Punjab. Unfortunately for India, the conditions are that people are apathetic even about things that concern them as a society. The methods adopted for *referendum* are new to them. Probably, the voters knew nothing of the fact that there was a *referendum* being taken about total prohibition. Mr King must have known the fact which everyone knows who knows anything of India that the vast majority of the people of India do not drink and that drinking intoxicants is contrary to Islam and Hinduism. The inference therefore to be drawn from the so-called failure referred to by Mr King is not that the Punjab is against the total prohibition but that the Punjabis being themselves as a class teetotallers do not bother their heads about those who are ruining themselves through the drink curse. He is also entitled to draw the inference that the Municipal commissioners and the members of the Local Boards have been criminally negligent of their duties to the voters in this matter of great social importance. But to argue from the facts cited that the Punjab is opposed to total prohibition is to throw dust in the eyes of strangers or ignorant people. That unfortunately is the way of the officials. Instead of looking at things impartially or from the popular standpoint, they constitute themselves pleaders for what the Government stands or for methods which the Government may wish to defend at any cost. It is a well-known fact that the Hindus are against the slaughter of the cow and her progeny. Supposing there was a *referendum* taken precisely in the manner in which it was taken in the Punjab regarding drink and the millions of Hindus fail to register their vote, will any one who knows Indian conditions argue therefrom, for one moment, that Hindus want slaughter-houses where the sacred cow is done to death? The fact is that there is not that consciousness created amongst the people that is impatient of social wrongs. It is no doubt a deplorable thing. It is being gradually mended. But it is a wicked thing to suppress facts which would warrant an inference totally different from the one that may in the absence of those facts, be drawn from another set of facts.

Young India, 8-4-'26

10

TOTAL PROHIBITION

> "I ask you to realize the fact that the alteration of the present Abkari Act with regard to making, manufacture and possession of liquor etc., must necessarily, to a large extent, lead to harassing of the people. You must be prepared for such a harassment which is an inevitable concomitant of the policy of prohibition. I must count then upon your unstinted support. I do not want your support for picketing shops, to preach about the evils of drink and other kindred work. But I want your help in the matter of putting down illicit manufacture of liquor and kindred crimes."

This is an extract from the speech of the Madras Minister for Public Health and Excise reported in the *Hindu*. There is one more assistance the Minister has asked the people to render, i.e. submit to increased taxation. Of this I do not propose at present to say anything except that where the people are able, they should submit to further taxation on proof of necessity. No monetary cost is too great to pay for achieving total prohibition.

But at the present moment, I would confine myself to the extract quoted by me. I fear that the Minister has taken a wrong view of prohibition. In my opinion, it has not to be taken piecemeal. To be successful it should be taken as a whole. It is not a one-district question but it is an all-India question.

What pains me about the Minister's speech is his superficial treatment of a question which affects the well-being of the masses. Surely he is not serious about his scheme if he expects the people to do his police work. And why does he frighten the people by saying that there must be harassment if prohibition is tried? Is there harassment of the people because theft or manufacture of gunpowder are classed as crimes? Is not unlicensed distillation even now a crime? What the Minister implies therefore is that the men who today hold licences to manufacture or sell liquor will, after the prohibition, distil surreptitiously and that therefore they will be harassed. There need be in this no harassment of the people.

But it betrays want of imagination and lack of sympathy with the people, if the Minister believes that as a prohibitionist he has nothing more to do but to declare prohibition and prosecute those who will break his laws. I venture to submit that prosecutions are the smallest and the destructive part of prohibition. I suggest that there is a larger and constructive side to prohibition. People drink because of the conditions to which they are reduced. It is the factory labourers and others that drink. They are forlorn, uncared for, and they take to drink. They are no more vicious by nature than teetotallers are saints by nature. The majority of people are controlled by their environment. Any Minister who is sincerely anxious to make prohibition a success will have to develop the zeal and qualities of a reformer. He will then require precisely the help that the Madras Minister is reported to have scorned. In my humble opinion, he does need pickets and men and women who would 'preach about the evils of drink' and do 'other kindred work'. It is just in these very things that he will want an army of volunteers who will be associated with him in reforming the life of the drunkard. He will have to convert every drink shop into a refreshment shop and concert room combined. Poor labourers will want some place where they can congregate and get wholesome, cheap, refreshing, non-intoxicating drinks, and if they can have some good music at the same time, it would prove as a tonic to them and draw them. These can by judicious management and association of the people become paying concerns for the State. He who will handle the problem of temperance will have to give a more serious study to it than the Minister seems to have done.

Young India, 8-9-'27

11

PROHIBITION AND NON-VIOLENCE

To

The Editor, *Young India*

Sir,

Surely Mr Rajagopalachari's scheme on p. 112 of your issue for the 4th April is inconsistent with Mr Gandhi's dogma of non-violence. Prohibition is force, and force is no remedy for anything, least of all for intemperance, especially among those who repudiate the use of force (violence) in any shape. 'Non-violent' prohibition is self-contradictory. Could one frame a section of the Penal Code to the effect that any one drinking a glass of toddy (or beer) in his own house shall be liable to fine or imprisonment ? I am altogether in favour of real temperance, but equally opposed to tyranny, and the prohibition of moderate (quite temperate) drinking is nothing but tyranny.

Yours truly,

6-5-1929 J. B. Pennington

I hold drinking spirituous liquors in India to be more criminal than the petty thefts which I see starving men and women committing and for which they are prosecuted and punished. I do tolerate, very unwillingly it is true and helplessly because of want of full realization of the law of love, a moderate system of penal code. And so long as I do, I must advocate the summary punishment of those who manufacture the fiery liquid and those even who will persist in drinking it notwithstanding repeated warnings. I do not hesitate forcibly to prevent my children from rushing into fire or deep waters. Rushing to red water is far more dangerous than rushing to a raging furnace or flooded stream. The latter destroys only the body, the former destroys both body and soul.

Young India, 8-8-'29

12

A GENTLE REBUKE

C. Rajagopalachari's eagle eye sees everything that appears in print about the drink evil. He saw a report of my very innocent speech at the village of Maroli * where the other day I laid the foundation of a weaving institute. I had there attempted to show the connection that exists between factory labour and drink and said how Mithubehn Petit had, whilst doing prohibition work, discovered that if the people who ceased to visit the liquor shops she picketed were to be permanently weaned from drink, they should have some ambition provided in life, some work found for them during their idle hours. I then showed how she found such occupation in hand-spinning and weaving. I further went on to show that if people had to do excessive labour, they would want some stimulant and illustrated it by an experience from my own life when during the Boer War I had to issue from the commissariat rations of rum for those bearers who were used to drink and who pleaded with me for rum which, they said, would enable them to bear the fatigue and resume next day's march. Of course, this was a superstition. But superstitions die hard.

Rajagopalachari feared that the report that he had read would be distorted to yield all kinds of meanings favourable to the opponents of prohibition. His fear has been justified. I have received embarrassing congratulations on my conversion to sanity. They embarrass me because I am not conscious of the conversion imputed to me. I feel like a man who falsely reported to have died reads his obituary notices and blushes to have the virtues he never knew he had possessed.

Let me therefore re-declare my faith in undiluted prohibition before I land myself in deeper water. If I was

* Maroli is a small village about 12 miles from Surat in the South.

appointed dictator for one hour for all India, the first thing I would do would be to close without compensation all the liquor shops, destroy all the toddy palms such as I know them in Gujarat, compel factory owners to produce humane conditions for their workmen and open refreshment and recreation rooms where these workmen would get innocent drinks and equally innocent amusements. I would close down the factories if the owners pleaded want of funds. Being a teetotaller I would retain my sobriety in spite of the possession of one hour's dictatorship and therefore arrange for the examination of my European friends and diseased persons who may be in medical need of brandy and the like at State expense by medical experts and where necessary, they would receive certificates which would entitle them to obtain the prescribed quantity of the fiery waters from certified chemists. The rule will apply *mutatis mutandis* to intoxicating drugs.

For the loss of revenue from drinks, I would straightway cut down the military expenditure and expect the Commander-in-Chief to accommodate himself to the new condition in the best way he can. The workmen left idle by the closing of factories, I would remove to model farms to be immediately opened as far as possible in the neighbourhood of the factories unless I was advised during that brief hour that the State could profitably run the factories under the required conditions and could therefore take over from the owners.

Young India, 25-6-'31

2. IN INDIAN STATES

13

ABKARI

The Princes' imitation of the British Abkari Department in order to increase their revenue is particularly distressing. It is said that Abkari is an ancient curse in India. I do not believe it to be so in the sense in which it is put. Princes in ancient times perhaps derived some revenue from the liquor traffic, but they never made the people the slaves of drink that they are now. Even granting that I am wrong and that Abkari in its present form has been in existence from times immemorial, still I do not subscribe to the superstition that everything is good because it is ancient. I do not believe either that anything is good because it is Indian. He who runs may see that opium and such other intoxicants and narcotics stupify a man's soul and reduce him to a level lower than that of beasts. Trade in them is demonstrably sinful. Indian States should close all liquor shops and thus set a good example for the British administrators to follow.

Young India, 8-1-'25

14

AN APPEAL

The reader will find something about Kali Paraj in my usual weekly notes. Many outside Gujarat may not know the meaning of Kali Paraj. It literally means black people. The name seems to have been given to a portion of the people of Gujarat by those who regarded themselves as superior to them. So far as colour is concerned the Kali Paraj are no blacker than or different from the rest. But today they are down-trodden, helpless, superstitious and timid. Their great vice is drink. By far the largest number of them belong to the Baroda State.

It was among these people that a great awakening came three years ago. Thousands left off drink and even flesh-eating. This proved too much for the liquor dealers. Most of these were Parsis. It is said that they tried all the means possible to induce the teetotallers to revert to drink and that they succeeded to a great extent. The officials too are said to have conspired against the reformers. And now whether as a result of these efforts or otherwise, there has sprung up among these people a party who teach them to regard temperance as a sin, and by ostracism and other means seek to break the spirit and the zeal of those who are battling against themselves and an evil habit handed down from generation to generation.

One of the resolutions passed at the meeting of which I have taken a fairly long notice elsewhere was to ask the States of Baroda, Dharampur and Bansda and also the British Government to close down all liquor shops. This is a big order, it will be said. The attempt of a whole nation to bring about total prohibition, it will be added, failed miserably. How then can the ineffective appeal of a handful of helpless men and women succeed ? There is a great deal of force in the argument. And yet the two attempts stand on a different footing. The attempt of 1921 was directed against the British Government by non-co-operators who were bent on wresting power from the Government. It was moreover directed by those who had not themselves suffered from the existence of liquor shops. Now the appeal comes from those who have been a prey to the evil. It is an appeal from the powerless to the powerful. It is addressed to all the governments concerned and not merely to the British Government. These men are no non-co-operators. They do not know the difference between co-operation and non-co-operation. They slave for others unwillingly, almost unknowingly, and often under fear of oppression. They do not know what Swaraj is. To them giving up drink and removal of the temptation in the shape of liquor shops is Swaraj. Their appeal therefore is on humanitarian grounds and should prove irresistible.

As President, I am bound to give effect to their resolution addressed to the governments concerned. The appeal to the British Government can only be through the legislators. It is open to the councillors to forgo the liquor revenue even though they may have to run the risk of starving the education department. I invite them to see the people themselves and have an ocular demonstration of the evil that is corrupting a whole race of men and women. They must dare to do the right thing if they will save their countrymen.

It is different with the States of Baroda, Dharampur and Bansda. They can, if they will, shut up the liquor shops and save their people and themselves from destruction. I use the pronoun 'themselves' deliberately, because the destruction of a large body of people in small States means their own destruction. Will they not listen to the appeal of those who want to be helped against themselves?

Young India, 22-1-'25

15

THE DRINK CURSE IN TRAVANCORE

The one thing most deplorable next to untouchability is the drink curse. The total excise revenue of the State was in 1922, Rs 46,94,300 against Land Revenue Rs 38,18,652 and out of a total revenue of Rs 1,96,70,130. This I regard as a most serious blot upon the administration. That so much of its revenue should be derived from intoxicants affords food for serious reflection. The excise revenue subdivides itself thus:

Abkari	.. ..	Rs 26,82,367
Opium & Ganja	.. ..	Rs 3,11,635
Tobacco	.. ..	Rs 17,00,298
	Total ..	Rs 46,94,300

Thus the liquor revenue is a terrific item. I was told that drink was most prevalent among the Christians and that it was decimating hundreds of homes and bringing poverty and disgrace upon thousands of men otherwise able and intelligent. From all one can see, the State is looking upon the increasing revenue with philosophic calmness, if not pleasure. The communities are playing with the evil and playing at temperance. It is necessary to stamp out the evil before it is too late. The most effective method no doubt is to make the getting of liquor impossible except upon a medical prescription. How to give up the largest source of revenue is the question. If I was the autocrat able to impose my will upon Travancore, I would remove that source of revenue altogether and close every liquor shop, take a census of those who are addicted to the habit and find out means of giving them healthy refreshments and healthy amusement or employment as the case may be and rely upon the people turned sober contributing to the revenue more by their increased efficiency than by drinking. But the days of autocracy are over. Democracy is the autocrat. The Legislative Council and the popular Assembly can do the whole thing. It would be wrong to fling one stone at the Maharani Regent and another at the Dewan and say that the duty was done. The people are having a daily increasing share in the administration of the State. They are extremely well-educated. They can force the State to use the whole of the revenue while it is being received, towards the eradication of the evil and insist upon closing the nefarious traffic in a year's time. But whether it can be done in a year or it must take longer is for the people to decide. Let them know that there is a snake in the grass. And I respectfully ask once more, who can lead in this matter if not the Christians? My importunity to the Christians does not absolve either the Hindus or the Mussalmans. But in such matters the first appeal must be to the stronger party.

Young India, 26-3-'25

16

IN DEFENCE

To,

The Editor, *Young India,*
Ahmedabad.

Sir,

In the course of an article on Travancore published in your esteemed paper, Mr M. K. Gandhi refers to the drink evil and says, giving some facts and figures :

"From all one can see the State is looking upon the increasing revenue with philosophic calmness, if not with pleasure."

I am afraid that the above statement is thoroughly unfounded and only justifies the statement that the observations of a few hours' world tourists are incorrect as they are formed on ill-informed data. I shall only place some facts and leave you and your readers to form their own impressions. These are culled from the report published last week of a Committee of officials and non-officials appointed by His Highness' Government to submit their proposals to enable Government to attain success in their declared policy of prohibition by slow and easy stages. So long ago as 1874, the then Dewan, Sir A. Seshiah Sastri in reviewing the excise revenue, said : "The increase in revenue under this head, though attributable directly to keen competition and indirectly to the increasing prosperity of the lower classes is, however, not a fit subject for congratulation in respect of its influence on the morals of the people and it were devoutly to be wished it were otherwise." During the past 50 years, the policy of Government has been to reduce the drink evil. In the year 1084 (1909), the figures stood thus :

"Kind of shops	No.	Area served per shop per sq. mile	Population served per shop
Arrack shops	677	5.67	2,822
Toddy shops	1,540	2.43	1,240
Arrack and Toddy shops	4,320	.76	240
"Four years later, the corresponding figures were :			
Arrack shops	735	9.55	4,665
Toddy shops	1,553	4.49	2,193
"In 1098 (1923), again the figures were :			
Arrack shops	631	11	6,287
Toddy shops	1,378	5.06	2,860

"Thus the policy of reducing the number of shops has been steadily maintained. Nor was it otherwise with regard to the taxation of intoxicating liquors. The duty of 7 annas per 20° u.p. or 8¾ as per proof gallon which prevailed in 1049 (1874), now stands at Rs 3 as. 12 per proof gallon showing an increase of 585.7 per cent, while the tree tax which stood at Re 1, 1½ and 2 for six months for a Palmyra, Cocoanut and *Choondapana* tree respectively in 1082 (1907) now stands at Re 1-12-0, Rs 3 and Rs 5 respectively. The strength of liquor has been reduced from 29° u.p. and 35° u.p. to 25° u.p. and 30° u.p." (Page 6, Excise Committee Report). This restrictive policy has largely been responsible for the reduction in the consumption of liquor. To quote the Excise Committee Report again:

"Whereas in 1088 (1913), the consumption of arrack stood at 1,16,624.95 proof gallons, in 1098 (1923) after a lapse of ten years, the consumption has been only 1,20,786.62 proof gallons. The consumption per head of population was only 1.46 drams in 1098, against 1.64 drams in 1088 (1913), that is to say, the consumption actually fell by 11.3 per cent when calculated on the increase in the population during the period....During the intervening period between 1088 and 1098, the population has increased by about 17 per cent" (page 6). In the face of these bare facts, it is for your readers to judge whether "the State is looking upon the increasing revenue with philosophic calmness, if not with pleasure". For further particulars about the measures taken to minimize the drink evil, I would refer you to *The Times of India* of 31st March, 1925.

A Travancorean

I was not unprepared for some such defence. But I remain unrepentant. I have paid unstinted tribute to the Travancore administration. But the *Abkari* policy admits of no such defence. The extracts quoted read like pages from British Administration reports. Liquor is not a matter to trifle with. No soft and easy-going policy will cope with the tremendous evil. Nothing short of total prohibition can save the people from the curse.

Young India, 16-4-'25

17

TEMPERANCE REFORM

For some time past, some Christians of Travancore have been earnestly striving to put down the drink habit by working from within, i.e., by seeing and speaking to the people given to the habit. They are trying to organize picketing with the intention of warning the visitors to the liquor dens. This simple procedure seems to have frightened the Travancore authorities. The District Magistrate at Kottayam has served a gagging notice upon Dr. Z. M. Paret who is a well-known Christian in Travancore and, so far as I know, whose non-violent spirit has never been questioned. This is the notice:

> "Whereas it has been made to appear to me from reports received from the District Superintendent of Police, Kottayam, that you are making speeches inciting people to do picketing before liquor shops and to commit other form of lawlessness and that speeches are likely to cause breaches of the peace and bring the authority of Government into contempt, I do hereby strictly order and enjoin you under Section 26 of the Regulation IV of 1095 not to make any speech, harangue or address from this day in any part of this District of Kottayam."

The notice begs the question by describing every speech advising picketing as an incitement. What 'the other form of lawlessness' can be is not made clear in the order. Thus in Travancore if the Magistrate's order correctly interprets its law, a premium is put upon the vice of drunkenness. Not only does a State provide facilities for drink but it also prevents reformers from resorting to the only effective and peaceful method of directly approaching the drunkards and appealing to them not to give way to temptation. I hope that the law of Travancore is faultless and that the District Magistrate has erred in his interpretation. The interpretation should be tested in a higher court. In any case, the reformers' duty is clear. If the law is at fault, they must move for its repeal. And if all effort to set it right fails, their peaceful picketing must go on even at the risk of being imprisoned, taking care to avoid enlisting as volunteers persons who cannot restrain themselves under provocation. It is worthy of note that the gag is perpetual.

Young India, 18-11-'26

18

A WELCOME STEP

A correspondent from Holalkere in Mysore writes:

> "I am highly glad to inform you that the people belonging to Lambani community of my taluk have completely abstained from drinking toddy and other liquors since a month and a half. It was in the Lambani Conference held in this town at the end of last April that they had taken an oath not to touch any liquor, prostrating themselves before the evening sun. Since then, they have not swerved from their oath. If any one of that community is seen near a toddy shop, he is strictly dealt with by the Naik, Yajaman and Karabhan of that hamlet. Their women carry to us every day the glad news, there are no broils at their hovel and that they lead a very peaceful life. This is an instance to show that your movement of purification had entered our State even before your entering it."

I congratulate the Lambani community upon the great step they have taken, and hope that they will not slide back like many who did so after the exultation of 1921 had subsided. Let me invite the attention of the leaders of the community to the case recorded in these pages of the Raniparaj people of whom those abstainers who took to *charkha* as a means of occupying their time and attention, not only had no hankering after liquor but were able to double their savings. For, they not only saved what was spent upon the drink but they also added to their income by saving in the cost of clothing. It is the universal experience of temperance reformers that if the people who take pledges do not usefully occupy their time, the hankering returns and it becomes too strong to resist the temptation. I hope too that other villages will follow the example of Holalkere and that when I am enabled to begin my tour in Mysore, I shall receive, side by side with glowing accounts which I have been promised of the progress of *khadi*, accounts also of eradication of the drink habit.

Young India, 16-6-'27

19

RANIPARAJ INQUIRY COMMITTEE

The Committee visited eighteen villages recording statements of witnesses from 47 villages in the Chikhli and Bulsar Talukas and in the State of Bansda. It reflects credit upon the Bansda State that the Committee is able to give a glowing account of the interest that the Maharaja Saheb of Bansda is taking in his people. But all the good that is undoubtedly being done by His Highness to his people, is really undone so long as he considers it necessary to derive an income from the drink traffic. No doubt the fact that the three neighbours adjacent to the Bansda territory, that is the British, the Gaekwad and Dharampur, have no prohibition makes it difficult for Bansda to carry out the policy of successful prohibition. But great things cannot be done without great sacrifice and great measures. Bansda cannot only lead the way by declaring out-and-out prohibition, but can then agitate for prohibition in the neighbouring States. The chief thing is to be prepared to sacrifice the drink revenue. An immediate beginning can be made by deciding not to use that revenue for any purpose however laudable it may be, save for that of carrying on an intensive anti-drink propaganda amongst the tribes given to drink. For, there is no doubt that any State that seriously wants its people to give up the evil habit cannot be satisfied merely with making it legally impossible to indulge in the evil habit, but to find out the causes of the habit and to educate the people to give it up. In the end, no State need suffer by depriving itself of the drink revenue. The inevitable outcome of any policy of prohibition carried out side by side with constructive work of the nature suggested by me must result in an ever increasing prosperity of the people and therefore of the State.

Young India, 16-6-'27

3. IN BURMA

20

MESSAGE TO THE BURMESE LAITY

"I was intensely pained," said Gandhiji at Moulmein, "to learn yesterday that the drink evil was on the increase and that the drink revenue amounted to one-third of the land revenue. It is a terrific thing to contemplate for any country in the world, but it is nothing less than suicidal in a country like Burma where climatic conditions are totally opposed to the drink habit. I know what the habit is doing in India. A serious responsibility rests on the shoulders of people living in towns. I would like the leaders of public opinion in Burma to consider this thing seriously and make every endeavour to root this thing out. Whatever may be true of countries with cold climates I am sure that in a climate like ours there is no need for drink whatsoever. Nothing but ruin stares a nation in the face that is a prey to the drink habit. History records that empires have been destroyed through that habit. We have it in India that the great community to which Shri Krishna belonged was ruined by that habit. This monstrous evil was undoubtedly one of the contributory factors in the fall of Rome. If therefore you will live decently you will shun this evil whilst there is yet time."

Young India, **11-4-'29**

21

LEGISLATION BEFORE EDUCATION

The Burma Women's Christian Temperance Union availed itself of the presence of Gandhiji in Rangoon to have him address a meeting of the Union. Miss May Mack, who was in the chair while welcoming Gandhiji remarked that their organization had been more and more recognizing the fact that temperance education must precede temperance legislation in order that the latter might be effective. She therefore suggested that what was needed in Burma was an intensive educational campaign amongst adults of all races stressing the necessity for total abstinence on the part of individuals. For no shop could remain long open if it ceased to be patronized.

Gandhiji replying said :

" You, madam, have suggested that if an educative campaign is carried on amongst the people, and as a consequence of that propaganda people who are in the habit of drinking cease to visit liquor shops, there would be no liquor shops in existence. I want to put before you my own experience without combating your view.

Conditions in South Africa

" My work in connection with temperance began as early as 1893 when I went to South Africa. When I saw my own people, my own countrymen drinking and even women drinking who would never think of drinking in India and as a result leading a life of the gutter, I saw that the task was an uphill one. These men and women were not prepared to listen to any lectures on temperance, much less to any personal advice. I saw too that some of them were perfectly helpless or they thought that they were helpless. I adopted many measures, all such measures as were within the competence of a man who is without any authority. But I cannot claim any degree of visible success for those efforts. There was a kind of a 'Liquor Commission' appointed by the Union Government after South Africa became a Union. I gave evidence or rather wrote a note for that

Commission, but I am again sorry to have to inform you that nothing came out of it. The position in South Africa was and still remains somewhat curious and anomalous. There are three different degrees of restriction on the possession and drinking of liquor. The Bantus and the Zulus are prohibited from carrying bottles with them or from being served in canteens, and yet they do drink. Indians may not possess bottles, but they may drink as much as they like in the canteens, with the result especially to the women that I have described to you. The white man is of course free. There is no legislation in connection with him, but you may guess what I would like to say. It is that the source of all this evil comes from this freedom of the white men in South Africa. Some of them have amassed a fortune by exploiting the drink habit of the Bantus and the Indians.

What Happened in India

"Then I came to India, and I found the position very different from the position in South Africa in one respect, but the problem was essentially the same. There was as you are aware a hurricane temperance campaign in 1920-21. And you will not mind my saying to you that if we had then received whole-hearted support from all the temperance organizations throughout the length and breadth of India, we would have achieved complete success. If you are careful students of the temperance movement in India you would gain the knowledge from the Government reports that we were within an ace of complete success, at least in some provinces. Many of the liquor dens were practically closed. Hundreds of opium dens in Assam were deserted. And then followed the tragedy. It consisted in Government repression. It was a shameful and sorry affair. I admit that the movement had a political colour. It was bound to have that political colour. But the political motive should not have deterred temperance organizations from helping a movement that was essentially moral. You will pardon me for taking you through this history which, if it is tragic, is also deeply interesting. The repression came about in this fashion. The Government revenue dwindled down at once in Bihar, in Assam, in the Central Provinces. There was an onrush of feeling, a desire, a yearning for self-purification.

That yearning came, I do not know how — we do not always know the mysterious ways in which God works. But there is the fact that the political movement became also a movement of self-purification, and in that onrush thousands of workers became volunteers to picket liquor shops and opium dens and the people also began to believe that it was their duty to desert the drinking booths. The Government started repression and thousands of volunteers were thrown into jails for the offence of picketing drink and drug shops with the result that today all those canteens that were deserted and opium dens that were almost closed are, I am afraid, doing probably the same volume of business as they were doing prior to 1920-21.

Legislation Must Precede Education

"The moral that I would like to draw from this story is that in this connection in India and Burma — treating Burma as a separate entity for our argument — legislation has really to go hand in hand with educative propaganda if not to precede it. I have not been able to study as carefully as I would like to have done the drink habit of the Burman. I assure you that ever since I have come into touch with Burmese opinion I am trying to learn from Burmese friends about this drink habit of the Burman, but I can speak about it only from second-hand evidence as against India about which I can speak from first-hand knowledge. And I am here before you to give my own evidence that drinking is not a habit with the aristocracy, certainly not with the middle class man ; it is a habit confined to the labourers and especially to the factory hands. And this is an interesting piece of evidence that I am placing before you. Why do factory hands drink when they did not drink before they came to work in the factories, even as those men and women who went to work in South Africa were not drinking before they migrated there ? The answer is that the conditions there are such and temptations that are placed in their way are such that they become addicted to the habit of drink. But even these men who have become addicted to the habit of drink do not justify it. They have a sense of shame about it. If you speak to them about it, they will tell you they are helpless, they are labourers ; they will tell you all sorts of falsehoods and try to deceive you, but they are ashamed of this habit. In Europe it will be ungentlemanly on my part if I do not stand a drink when you come to see me. When I was a student in England, I found myself in a most embarrassing position because I would not stand a drink to friends. But that is not the case in India, and therefore I suggest that it would be a wrong thing for you to say that education has to precede legislation. Education will never be able to cope with the evil. There is no prohibition because drink brings a large revenue. Even Indian Ministers say, 'We cannot forgo this revenue, you must go on educating.'

"I would therefore appeal to you, especially the women, who are concerned with temperance work to take courage in both your hands. I do not ask you to take as gospel truth what I have told you. Test the truth for yourselves and if you find that what I have told you is more than confirmed by your investigations, then I suggest that you will make it your sacred duty to carry on a whirlwind campaign for total prohibition. The task is difficult only because the rights that have been created through the drink evil belong to the ruling race.

The Reformer's Position

"If you discuss this problem with the administrators, they will tell you all sorts of stories and put all manner of difficulties in the way of carrying this legislation through. Do not believe these difficulties at all. There is no difficulty at all beyond the difficulty of making up the deficit of revenue. If you and I have made up our minds that this evil has got to be eradicated and if it can be eradicated only by prohibition legislation, then it is for the Government to find a way out of the deficit difficulty. It is not open to it to ask you to suggest ways and means for making up that deficit. That would be like the conduct of man who comes to you with unclean hands and asks you to help him to clean them. However there is a question of picketing. When the psychological moment comes, — and I am praying for that moment, — when every liquor shop and opium den is picketed, I will expect you to lend a helping hand and not to say, 'How can we help him ? He is an agitator.' Even now an intensive agitation for temperance is being carried on in the Surat district, and that has been possible because there is a band of workers including women belonging to cultured families, self-sacrificing and brave. When we have got a compact body of reliable and unimpeachable workers we shall carry on this campaign over the whole country. And when that time comes you will find the whole of India dotted with pickets and I hope that that influence will percolate through the Bay of Bengal to Burma. Burmese ladies and gentlemen too may then, if they so choose, carry on picketing and thus save a noble race from extinction which so far as I can see stares them in the face — as much as it does India — if they are not weaned from this curse in time."

Young India, 18-4-'29

B. UNDER CONGRESS GOVERNMENTS

22

PROHIBITION CRITICISM ANSWERED

How can total prohibition be brought about immediately if at all ? By 'immediately' I mean an immediate planned declaration bringing about total prohibition not later than three years from 14th July 1937, the date of the taking of office by the first Congress Ministry. I imagine that it is quite possible to bring it about in two years. But not being aware of administrative difficulties I put down three years. I count loss of this revenue as of no account whatsoever. Prohibition will remain a far cry, if the Congress is to count the cost in a matter of first class national importance.

Let it be remembered that this drink and drugs revenue is a form of extremely degrading taxation. All taxation to be healthy must return tenfold to the tax-payer in the form of necessary services. Excise makes people pay for their own corruption, moral, mental and physical. It falls like a dead-weight on those who are least able to bear it. The revenue is largely derived, I believe, from industrial labour which together with field labour the Congress almost exclusively represents.

The loss of revenue is only apparent. Removal of this degrading tax enables the drinker, i.e. the tax-payer to earn and spend better. Apart, therefore, from the tremendous gain, it means a substantial economic gain, to the nation.

I put this prohibition in the forefront because its result is immediate ; Congressmen and especially women have bled for it ; national prestige will rise in a manner it cannot by any single act that I can conceive, and the other five provinces are highly likely to follow the six. The Mussalman non-Congress Prime Ministers are equally interested in seeing India sober rather than drunk.

The cry of great expenditure in preventing illicit distillation is thoughtless where it is not hypocritical. India is not America. The American example is a hindrance rather than a help to us. In America drinking carries no shame with it. It is the fashion there to drink. It reflects the greatest credit on the determined minority in America that by sheer force of its moral weight it was able to carry through the prohibition measure however short-lived it was. I do not regard that experiment to have been a failure. I do not despair of America once more returning to it with still greater fervour and better experience in dealing with it. It may be that if India carries out prohibition it will hasten the advent of prohibition in America. In no part of the world is prohibition as easy to carry out as in India for with us it is only a minority that drinks. Drinking is generally considered disrespectable. And there are millions, I believe, who have never known what drink is.

But why should prevention of illicit distillation cost any more than prevention of other crimes ? I should make illicit distillation heavily punishable and think no more about it. Some of it will go on perhaps till Doomsday as thieving will. I would not set up a special agency to pry into illicit distilleries. But I would punish anyone found drunk though not disorderly (in the legal sense) in streets or other public places with a substantial fine or alternatively with indeterminate imprisonment to end when the erring one has earned his or her keep.

This, however, is the negative part. Voluntary organizations especially manned by women will work in the labour areas. They will visit those who are addicted to drink and try to wean them from the habit. Employers of labour will be expected by law to provide cheap, healthy refreshment, reading and entertainment rooms where the working men can go and find shelter, knowledge, health-giving food and drink and innocent fun.

Thus prohibition means a type of adult education of the nation and not merely a closing down of grog shops.

Prohibition should begin by preventing any new shop from being licensed and closing some that are in danger of becoming a nuisance to the public. How far the latter is possible without having to pay heavy compensation I do not know. In any case, generally, licences that lapse should not be renewed. No new shops should be opened on any account. Whatever immediately is possible in law should be done without a moment's thought so far as the revenue is concerned.

But what is the meaning or extent of total prohibition ? Total prohibition is prohibition against sales of intoxicating drinks and drugs, except under medical prescription by a practitioner licensed for the purpose and to be purchasable only at Government depots maintained therefor. Foreign liquors in prescribed quantity may be imported for the use of Europeans who cannot or will not do without their drink. These will also be sold in bottles in select areas and under authorized certificates. Hotels and restaurants will cease to sell intoxicating drinks.

Harijan, 31-7-'37

23

AGAINST AHIMSA AND TRUTH?

A friend writes:

"The following sentence in your article 'Criticism Answered' (31st July) seems to me to offend against the spirit of truth and non-violence as also against good logic.

'Foreign liquors in prescribed quantity may be imported for the use of Europeans who cannot or will not do without their drink.'

The Congress Governments must feel as much concerned for the welfare of the European community within their provinces as for the Indian communities. I assume that the Congressmen, as prohibitionists, are all agreed that drink is as bad for the European as for the Indian. In that case, the mere whim of the drinker cannot count. If drink is to be allowed to the European — although it is bad for him — because 'he cannot or will not do without it' the Japanese, the Americans and several other foreigners in India may seek the same permission; and if they are to be allowed to continue their evil habit on that ground, why should an Indian in his own country be not allowed to ruin himself in the same way?

I think, therefore, that if drink is to be prohibited by the Congress Ministries, they would be unjust towards the Europeans if their welfare is thus sacrificed out of, apparently, a regard for their mental idiosyncracies. Surely, the permission to drink ought not to assume the form of a privilege to be conferred upon an individual, far less upon a community as a whole. If anyone is to be permitted to take, 'not take to', alcohol, it must be entirely on medical or some other universally applicable ground. There cannot be under the Congress regime a discriminatory legislation for or against a community.

History records that when the first Parsi settlers came to India, they agreed not only to respect but also to adopt certain of the Indian customs prevailing. The European merchants had to respect the manners and customs of the Moghul court. A foreigner domiciled in India would be equally obliged to do so. A foreigner residing in India for a period only ought not to be exempt from the same obligation. Thus, even for those who feel that total abstinence is not absolutely necessary, it must be obligatory to give up drink during their stay in India if the nation has declared itself against it. They must be deemed to reside in India on the understanding that they will respect the laws, customs and rules of decent conduct of the people amongst whom they have come to reside."

I have no difficulty generally in following and often adopting this writer's criticism. But I must confess that though I have read the letter three times, I have failed to understand the argument.

Why is the proposed exemption against the spirit of *ahimsa* or truth ? I fail to see even the bad logic the writer sees in it. In dealing with living entities, the dry syllogistic method leads not only to bad logic but sometimes to fatal logic. For if you miss even a tiny factor — and you never have control over all the factors that enter into dealings with human beings, — your conclusion is likely to be wrong. Therefore you never reach the final truth, you only reach an approximation, and that too if you are extra careful in your dealing.

Indeed, it was my regard for *ahimsa* and truth that made me think of exempting Europeans. For I am unable to lay down a universal law for all human beings and for all climes that drink is an evil. I can well regard it as a necessity in the frigid zone. I would therefore be chary of imposing prohibition against Europeans who not only do not regard measured quantities of alcohol at each meal an evil but consider it a necessity. Drink is not regarded as a vice in European society as it is generally in India. I would, therefore, even from the point of view of courtesy (a phase of *ahimsa*), leave it to their honour to respect the usage of the country of their adoption.

I would gladly accept the logic of allowing other nationals, if the necessity is proved, the modified freedom the Europeans will enjoy. Indeed it might be necessary to bring in a large number of Indians too under the medical certificate clause.

For me, the drink question is one of dealing with a growing social evil against which the State is bound to provide whilst it has got the opportunity. The aim is patent. We want to wean the labouring population and the Harijans from the curse. It is a gigantic problem, and the best resources of all social workers, especially women, will be taxed to the utmost before the drink habit goes. The prohibition I have adumbrated is but the beginning (undoubtedly indispensable) of the reform. We cannot reach the drinker so long as he has the drink shop near his door to tempt him. One might as well prevent an ailing child, nay man, from touching sweets so long as he does not remove the open box in front of them.

Whilst on this question, I would like to answer an argument advanced in one of the newspaper cuttings which good friends send me, that Shri C. Rajagopalachari in his zeal for this reform has brushed aside the question of the unemployment of the tappers who will be thrown out of work. I do not know what he has in mind for them. Shri Gajanan, who is becoming an expert in making palm *gur*, tells me that, in the Southern Presidency, there are tappers engaged in the nefarious trade. He further suggests that the tapping need not stop at all. Only what they will tap under the prohibition regime will be sweet toddy which will be converted into *gur* instead of the fiery liquid. Indeed, I learn that, in Andhradesh, the tappers do not sell the palm juice they extract, but they convert it into *gur* which they sell to the arrack manufacturers who make arrack out of this *gur*. In such cases, nothing need be done except for the State to take over this *gur* at a reasonable agreed price. From what I know of the tappers, they are not likely to lose anything by the impending prohibition, and the poor will get a rich but cheap food in the shape of good pure *gur* instead of a liquid which harms both body and soul.

Harijan, 14-8-'37

24

DANGEROUS EVEN IN FRIGID ZONE

Apropos of my remark that alcohol might be required in a frigid zone, a friend sends me the following interesting paragraph from *Liquor Control* by G. E. G. Catlin who while discussing the apparent warming effect of alcohol says:

> "A simple mechanical consideration should however, warn us against a misinterpretation of these results. The body temperature has not been changed but the warmer blood has been sent to the surface where, if it is chilled, it returns to reduce the temperature of the whole system. In cases where there is serious need of protection against cold, alcohol is not only useless but dangerous. Fridtjof Nansen stated that 'my experience leads me to take a decided stand against the use of stimulants and narcotics of all sorts' in Arctic journeys — in the case of alcohol owing to the increased risk of death by freezing."

We in India, however, do not need such testimony. We have no excuse apparent or real for taking alcoholic drinks in our temperate zone where the sun gives us all the warmth we need.

Harijan, 28-8-'37

25

THE GREATEST ACT

I regard this resolution (regarding Prohibition) as the greatest act of the Working Committee at any time of its chequered career. The cry of prohibition has been always fashionable. In 1920 it became one of the chief constructive items of the Congress. The Congress, therefore, could not but go in for total prohibition immediately it came into power in any part of India. The Ministers had to have the courage to sacrifice nearly rupees eleven crores of revenue in the six provinces. The Working Committee has taken the risk for the sake of redeeming its pledge and conserving the moral and the material welfare of those who are addicted to intoxicants and narcotics. It is my fervent hope that the five provinces which have non-Congress majorities will not hesitate to follow the example of the six provinces. It is less difficult for them than for the six provinces to achieve prohibition. And is it too much to expect the States to fall in with British India ?

I know that many are sceptical about prohibition being achieved. They think that the financial lure will be too strong for them to resist. They argue that the addicts will procure their drinks and drugs anyhow, and that when the Ministers discover that prohibition means mere loss of revenue without any appreciable diminution in the consumption, though illicit, of drinks and drugs, they will revert to the tainted revenue and the then state will be worse than the present.

I do not share any such fear. I believe there is the requisite moral momentum in the nation to achieve the noble end. If prohibition is to be a reality, we shall begin to see the end not with the end of the three years but inside of six months. And when the reality dawns upon India, those provinces or States that have lagged behind are bound to bow to the inevitable.

We have the right, therefore, to expect the sympathy and support not only of all the parties in India including the Europeans but the best mind of the whole world in this, perhaps, the greatest moral movement of the century.

If, then, prohibition is to mean a great moral awakening in India, the closing of liquor shops should merely mean the indispensable beginning of the movement ending in the complete weaning from drink and narcotics of those poor people and some rich people whom the habit has ruined, body and soul. Such a consummation cannot be brought about by mere State effort. At the risk of repetition of what is stated by Mahadev Desai in his notes let me summarize what should, in my opinion, be the comprehensive programme :

(1) A drink drug map showing the locality of liquor and opium shops in each province.

(2) Closing them as liquor shops on the expiry of the licences.

(3) Immediate earmarking of liquor revenue, whilst it is still being received, exclusively for the purposes of prohibition.

(4) Conversion, wherever possible, of the liquor shops into refreshment and recreation rooms in the hope that the original visitors will continue to use them, liquor contractors being themselves persuaded to conduct them if they will.

(5) Employment of the existing excise staff for detection of illicit distillation and drinking.

(6) Appeal to the educational institutions to devote a part of the time of teachers and students to temperance work.

(7) Appeal to the women to organize visits to the persons given to the drink and opium habits.

(8) Negotiation with the neighbouring States to undertake simultaneous prohibition.

(9) Engaging the voluntary or, if necessary, paid assistance of the medical profession for suggesting non-alcoholic drinks and other substitutes for intoxicants and methods of weaning the addicts from their habit.

(10) Revival of the activities of temperance associations in support of the campaign against drink.

(11) Requiring employers of labour to open and maintain under first class management refreshment, recreation and educational rooms for the use of their employees.

(12) Toddy tappers to be used for drawing sweet toddy for sale, as such, or conversion into *gur*. I understand that the process of collecting sweet toddy for drinking, as such, or for making *gur* is different from the one for fermenting toddy.

So much for the campaign against drink and drugs.

Now as to how to make up for the loss of revenue in some provinces to the extent of one-third ? I have unhesitatingly suggested cutting out the educational budget for which purpose mainly the excise revenue is used. I still maintain that education can be made self-supporting. With this I must deal elsewhere. It cannot be made so in a day even if the possibility of its being made self-supporting is accepted. Existing obligations have to be met. Therefore, fresh sources of revenue have to be tapped. Death duties, tax on tobacco including *bidis*, have already been given as some suggestions. If these are considered impossible of immediate accomplishment, short-term loans may be devised to tide over the deficit; and if even that fails, the Central Government should be approached to curtail the military budget and give the Provinces the proportionate grant. The demand would be irresistible especially if it is demonstrated by the Provincial Governments that they do not need the military, at any rate for their internal peace and tranquillity.

Harijan, 28-8-'37

26
NOT IMPRACTICABLE

Sardar Sir Jogendra Singh is a great social reformer, a man of letters and a politician. Whatever, therefore, he writes commands attention. He has contributed an article on Total Prohibition to *The Times of India*. Having read it with the care his writings demand from me, I must confess that I left the article with a sigh. How could such a reformer accept defeat on grounds that do not bear examination? His only argument seems to be, "There is bound to be illicit distillation and secret drinking, therefore do not attempt prohibition." In the Punjab there was local option but nobody applied it. "Therefore," he says, "my conclusion is that prohibition by compulsion will fail, and provinces will lose revenue which they need for rural re-construction." By linking prohibition to revenue, the Sardar has precipitately given up his case and contradicted himself. For in the fourth paragraph of his article, he says: "I expressly declared that considerations of revenue would not weigh with me in carrying out a policy of controlling drink." Thank God, Congress Ministries have cut their way through the revenue snare by debarring themselves from the use of liquor revenue. Once the loop-hole is left, the temptation to make use of this immoral gain will be too irresistible, for nobody denies the difficulty of making the drunkard sober in a moment. Old Ministers, with whom I used to plead for prohibition, did not put forth the plea of impracticability. But they pleaded inability to forgo the rich revenue received from the traffic. They wanted it for education. Is education paid for by a questionable source of revenue worth having ? Has it intrinsic merit ? Has India got her money's worth from those who have received the education of the type that the schools and colleges of India provide ?

Thieving will abide till Doomsday. Must it therefore be licensed ? Is thieving of the mind less criminal than thieving of matter ? Illicit distillation to an extent will no doubt go on. Its quantity will be the measure of the Government's effort assisted by a vigilant public in the shape of continuous and sympathetic treatment of the drinker and the opium eater. Moral elevation demands a price no less than material or physical elevation. But my submission is that this constructive effort is doomed to failure if it is not preceded by total prohibition. So long as the State not only permits but provides facilities for the addict to satisfy his craving, the reformer has little chance of success. Gipsy Smith was a powerful temperance preacher. It was a feature of his huge gatherings that several people took the vow of total abstinence under the spell of his song and precept. But I say from my experience of South Africa that the majority of the poor addicts could not resist the temptation to enter the palatial bars that faced them, no matter where they wandered in the principal thoroughfares of cities, or the wayside inns when they strayed away from cities. State prohibition is not the end of this great temperance reform, but it is the indispensable beginning of it.

Of local option the less said the better. Was there ever opposition to the closing of these dens of vice ? Option has a place where a whole population wants to drink.

God willing, prohibition has come to stay. Whatever other contribution may or may not be made by the Congress, it will go down to history in letters of gold that the Congress pledged itself to prohibition in 1920, and redeemed the pledge at the very first opportunity without counting the cost. I doubt not that the other provinces will follow. I invite Sardar Jogendra Singh not to caution the Congress against the much needed reform, but to throw in his full weight in favour of it in his own province and among the stalwart Sikhs.

Harijan, 25-9-'37

27

CONDITIONS OF SUCCESS

Bhausaheb Lavate has been honouring me with a visit in the interest of prohibition which is as dear to him as to me. We came to the following conclusions :

1. Strict non-use from now of all Excise Revenue for any but prohibition purposes.

2. Non-renewal of all licences on their expiry and immediate closing of all liquor shops, where there is a clear demand for closing on the part of at least 75 per cent of those who have been visiting these shops.

3. Liquor, whenever it is necessary to sell it, should be sold only through direct Government agency.

4. All existing liquor shops should be, wherever possible, converted into refreshment and recreation rooms.

5. Causes of the habit in typical areas should be carefully investigated and dealt with.

6. Absolutely peaceful, silent and educative picketing by recognized individuals or groups should be undertaken, the object being to establish intimate personal contact with the addicts so as to help them to give up the habit. Personal visits to the addicts in their own homes would be a feature of scientific picketing. Voluntary agency for this work should be invited by the Government and encouraged to do this philanthropic work.

Harijan, 9-10-'37

28

NOT TODDY BUT NIRA

Some persons are consciously or unconsciously imputing to me an approval of fermented toddy. I have made it perfectly plain that prohibition affects all intoxicating drinks and drugs without exception. Fermented toddy, therefore, can never be tolerated under any scheme of total prohibition. But what I have said and what I repeat is that sweet unfermented toddy, which is called *nira*, should not be prohibited, and that the drinking of it in the place of fermented toddy should be encouraged. How it can be done is for the Prohibition Ministers to determine.

Harijan, 30-10-'37

29

IS NIRA OBJECTIONABLE ?

Among the fourteen points that Parsi friends have raised against the prohibition campaign there occurs this strange passage :

> "Mahatmaji persuades the Parsis to drink *nira*, sweet unfermented toddy, but the Parsis very well know the properties of *nira*. Moreover the British Government had already tried this *nira* drinking experiment free of tree-tax, but it failed because *nira* produces cold, flatulence, diarrhoea, etc. The experiment was already tried in Mahatmaji's Ashram at Segaon and there fatal results were pronounced."

I do not know what the Bombay Government tried. But I do know what *nira* is doing and has done to those who are trying it. It is wholly wrong to say that the experiment at Segaon Ashram failed and that it produced fatal results. It has never been known to have produced any of the bad results ascribed to it by the writer. On the contrary, *nira* is still being freely drunk by many in Segaon and that with profit to their health. Moreover, it is turned into syrup or *gur*, and in that condition I and many others use it almost daily. As *gur* it is sold in large quantities. It is better relished than sugarcane *gur* because of its being less sweet. As to the deaths that occurred in Wardha, not in Segaon, the investigations have clearly showed that the deaths were due not to *nira* drinking but to cholera. Nothing has been shown to establish any connection between the deaths and *nira*. Supposing the patients had developed cholera without drinking *nira*, would it have been right to say that cholera was induced by the ordinary food that they had eaten ? I may mention that several people had taken in Segaon with impunity the same *nira* that had been taken in Wardha.

If the thirteen other points are based on as weak a foundation as this (No. 13) is, surely there is no case against prohibition. And I make bold to say that the rest are no stronger. I have picked out the thirteenth in the hope that my personal testimony may put the opponents on their guard against making statements they cannot substantiate. Opposition based on reason must always command respect. This one seems to me to lack that essential quality.

Brindaban, 7-5-'39
Harijan, 13-5-'39

30

USES OF MAHURA

A correspondent writes a long letter about *mahura* flowers, and desires that all restrictions on the use of *mahura* flowers, other than that for distillation, should be removed. As an out-and-out prohibitionist I have no hesitation in endorsing the proposal. The whole conception of prohibition is not penal but educative. As soon as State recognition of intoxicating drinks and drugs, and licensed shops for the sake thereof, is withdrawn, the way of education becomes clear. Pènal enactments under the prohibition law will have to be of a character wholly different from those that have hitherto been in vogue. People will be trusted, therefore, if my scheme is accepted, to make the right use of *mahura*, and not prevented from using it altogether from fear of wrong use. Therefore, under the prohibition law, there will be no check on the right use of *mahura*, as there will be none on the right use of toddy. The following are some of the uses of *mahura* flowers, *mahura* oil and *mahura* wood, which I copy from the letter :

1. Fresh *mahura* flowers are sweet to eat.
2. A variety of tasteful preparations are made out of dried *mahura* flowers. These preparations serve as sweets to the poor people.
3. Decoction of *mahura* flowers is very effective in removing chronic constipation.
4. The oil from the seed called *dolia* is used as food. It is the poor man's ghee.
5. *Mahura* flowers are regarded as tonic for both men and cattle.
6. In times of scarcity and famine, which are very frequent in Kheda *mahura* flowers go a long way in saving the poor from complete starvation.
7. *Dolia* oil is specially favoured in the preparation of washing soap.
8. *Mahura* wood is used as fuel and timber.

Harijan, 25-9-'37

31

MONSTROUS IF TRUE

A correspondent writes :

> "Here in Nasik there is a Police Training School. Police officers are made in this school. They are expected to have their meals in a common mess and they are obliged to partake of fleshmeat and wines. Let alone meat-eating, how far is it consistent with the prohibition policy of the Government to train its police officers in wine drinking ? These officers may well be required to take part in the prohibition drive. Perhaps you do not even know that meat-eating and wine drinking is compulsory in this school."

I must confess my ignorance of the compulsion. It is only the assurance with which my correspondent writes that has induced me to publish the letter. If the information is true, it is surely monstrous that meat-eating and wine drinking should be considered a necessary part of a police officer's training. This rule excludes vegetarians and non-drinkers from training as police officers. The rule is a grave injustice in a country in which tens of thousands are vegetarians by religion. I can only hope that the information is incorrect and that if it is true, the glaring wrong will be redressed without delay.

Harijan, 5-11-'38

32

PROHIBITION

Prohibition in the Congress provinces is not going on in the spirit in which it was conceived. It is perhaps no fault of the Ministers. Public opinion is not insistent. Congress opinion is equally dormant. Congressmen do not seem to see that prohibition means new life for many millions. It means new and substantial accession of moral and material strength. They do not realize that honest prohibition gives a dignity and prestige to the Congress which perhaps no other single step can give. They do not see that prosecution of prohibition means identification with the masses and a resolute determination to refuse to have anything to do with the drink revenue. Even such a confirmed prohibitionist like Rajaji has not had the daring to set apart the drink revenue purely for the purpose of fighting the drink evil. He has proved in this matter too cautious for me. Congressmen have learnt to count no cost too dear for winning freedom. Our freedom will be the freedom of slaves if we continue to be victims of the drink and drug habit. Is any cost too much to establish complete prohibition in all the provinces?

And yet one finds Ministers drawing up prohibition programmes in a proper *bania* spirit. They think of their deficits. I wonder what they will do if all the wine-bibbers and opium-eaters suddenly give up their drinks and drugs. They will manage somehow, it may be answered. Why will they not do so voluntarily? Surely, merit lies in doing the right thing voluntarily, not compulsorily. The Bihar Government did not come to a standstill, when the earthquake swallowed more than their annual income. What do the Governments all over India do, when famines and floods ruin people and materially reduce the State revenue? I maintain that the Congress Government break the spirit, if not the letter, of their pledge, when they delay prohibition for the sake of revenue.

They can and must make an honest attempt to raise money by fresh taxation. The drink curse is most prevalent in urban areas. It is in those areas that they can resort to fresh taxation. Prohibition gives direct help to the employers of labour. They can surely afford to bear the loss of revenue caused by prohibition. The few months of prohibition in Ahmedabad have put money into the pockets both of the employers and the labourers. There is no reason whatsoever why the employers should not pay for this inestimable service. Many similar sources of revenue can easily be thought of.

I have not hesitated to suggest a grant or at least a loan without interest from the Government of India where it can be proved that the raising of additional revenue is not a practical proposition.

The only valid reason for not having immediate prohibition is want of previous experience and hence the need for caution. I viewed the Salem experiment in that light. The Madras Government wanted to take the first step with great deliberation and did not want to take any risk of failure. The success of the Salem experiment should be sufficient encouragement to go on with the whole scheme. But it is not impossible to understand the desire of each Government to go in for prohibition in stages so as to have local experience. It was for that reason that the Working Committee fixed three years as the period to bring about complete prohibition. The time is running fast. And if India is to be free of the curse within the period fixed, there should be no delay for want of money or for fear of deficit in revenue. And if the programme is prosecuted with single-minded zeal, there is no doubt that the other provinces and the States will follow.

Segaon, 19-12-'38
Harijan, 24-12-'38

33

DRINKING METHYLATED SPIRITS

A correspondent writes:

"Perhaps it is not information to you but I will be erring on the safe side and am, therefore, writing to inform you that people having the drink habit drink diluted methylated spirits because they cannot get toddy and *daru*. A convenient intermediary purchases a bottle of the spirits for 6 to 7 annas, dilutes it with water and sells it to the drunkard for 12 to 13 annas. The intermediary is not a businessman. He is an ordinary person who finds prohibition handy inasmuch as it enables him to earn a little money by buying a few bottles of methylated spirits and retailing the same to the drunkard.

I do not know if it would be practicable to control the sale of methylated spirits by issuing licences for its purchases. A watch over the total quantity of methylated spirits and other substitutes for toddy and *daru* sold in particular areas before and after the introduction of prohibition would appear to be necessary."

The correspondent's letter deserves the attention of those who are engaged in prohibition work.

Bardoli, 16-1-'39

Harijan, 21-1-'39

34

MEANING OF PROHIBITION

(Extracts)

His Grace the Archbishop of Bombay has been kind enough to send me a letter and a copy of his address to the Rotary Club against prohibition. I have read both with the respect and attention their author deserves.

My study of His Grace's letter and address at once revealed a serious flaw for which I must be held primarily responsible. The word prohibition is a misnomer for what the Bombay Government and the other Provincial Governments where the Congress controls the Ministries are doing, regarding the liquor trade. What the Governments are in reality doing is not prohibiting drink but they are closing liquor shops which are absolutely under Government control. The shop-owners have no statutory protection save what they get from year to year. Every owner of a liquor shop knows that his licence may not be renewed next year. He may be even outbidden if he possesses a country liquor or toddy licence as these are auctioned every year. Therefore, the licensees have no vested interest in their licences beyond the year for which they are held and then too subject to the observance of the stringent conditions laid down for them. Therefore I claim that the law for the abolition of liquor licences "is an ordinance of reason for the common good, made and promulgated for the community by the competent authority." All that the State is doing is to remove from the drinker the temptation or the facility which the State considers is harmful to him except for medicinal purposes.

Attempts were made even in the days of non-co-operation to induce the authorities to undertake the abolition legislation. Without exception they pleaded financial inability, never the impropriety of so-called interference with the right of the people to be supplied with liquor by the State. Indeed one Minister told me that if I would help him to raise the revenue needed to make up for the loss caused by the drop in the drink revenue, he would introduce prohibition at once. It is an open secret that the reform has been delayed simply for the sake of the revenue. In other words, the people have been tempted to drink for the sake of raising the revenue. The black history of the opium trade bears out the truth of this statement.

Those who speak in the name of individual freedom do not know their India. There is as much right of a person to demand drinking facilities from the State as there is to demand facilities for the supply of public women for the satisfaction of his animal passion. I hope that those who pride themselves on their moderation in drinking will not feel hurt by the illustration I have taken. In this country, we are not used to legislation for the regulation of vice. But in countries like Germany, the houses of women who sell their virtues are licensed. I do not know what will be more resented in those countries, the stopping of the licences for the houses of ill fame or the houses of drink. When woman realizes her dignity, she will refuse to sell her virtue and those members of the sex who are jealous of its honour will move heaven and earth to have legalized prostitution abolished. Will it be then contended that such abolition will go hard with the prostitutes and their dependants whose only means of livelihood depended upon this calling ?

I plead that social workers cannot work effectively so long as licensed liquor dens continue to lure the drinkers to enter them.

Harijan, 17-6-'39

35

BOMBAY THE BEAUTIFUL

'Handsome is that handsome does' is a neat proverb. I have often said that it is wrong to call Bombay beautiful only because of the fine approach to the harbour or for its many beauty spots so long as it contains dirty chawls, over-crowded lanes and uninhabitable hovels which serve as dwelling places for its Harijans. But when Bombay goes dry, as it will very soon, it will become truly beautiful even for this one singularly beautiful act and it will deserve the title in spite of the blemishes I have mentioned. For when its labouring population has the temptation of drink removed from them, with the improvement in their condition which always follows the exorcism of the drink evil, it must become easier for the Bombay Municipality to deal with the problem of providing better habitations for the poor classes. The Bombay Government, and especially Dr. Gilder, deserve the thanks of the citizens of Bombay, nay of the whole Province, for the courage with which they have approached their task. I know that many Parsis who depend upon drink traffic for their living will be affected. Bombay is the stronghold of the Parsis. Then there are its fashionable citizens who think they need their spirituous drinks as they need water. I have every hope that they will all rise to the occasion, think of their poor brethren, even if they do not appreciate abstinence for themselves, and set an example to all India and make good the claim of Bombay not only to be beautiful but also the first city in India.

Prohibition in Bombay will mean a big fall in revenue. The Finance Minister has to balance his budget. He has to find money. He has to levy new taxes. Let there be no complaint from those who will have to bear the burden. Dislike of taxes, be they ever so reasonable, is proverbial. I understand that the Finance Minister has met all just objections. Why should those who will have to bear the burden not feel a pride in being given the privilege of contributing to the great experiment? It will be a proud day for Bombay if prohibition is ushered in amid the rejoicings of the whole population. Let it be remembered that this prohibition is not a superimposition. It is being introduced by Governments that are responsible to the people. It has been a plank in the national programme since 1920. It is coming, therefore, in due fulfilment of the national will definitely expressed nearly twenty years ago.

New Delhi, 26-3-'39
Harijan, 1-4-'39

36

BHANDARIS AND PROHIBITION

As the train taking me to the Frontier Province was steaming out the station, Rao Bahadur Bole handed me a copy of the petition of the Bhandaris of Bombay addressed to the Prime Minister. He pressed me to read it and send him my reply. I read the petition after resting my tired limbs and sent him my reply.

The petition is an interesting document and deserves public notice. According to it the Bhandaris got the concession to tap trees as early as 1672 as a mark of favour for military services rendered to the then British Power. Then they lost the concession. But they were able to continue their occupation, and to the present that is the occupation of about 8,000 people.

The petitioners say they are not against prohibition but they plead for gradualness extending to a few years.

Then comes the sting at the very tail-end. It runs: "If the Government fail to pay heed to all these entreaties and leave the Bhandaris to their fate as it falls upon them, we do not know what course these poorly educated and uneducated people may follow in their sheer disappointment. We are afraid they may even go to the length of adopting not only Congress methods of seeking relief but adopting more drastic measures in their frenzy."

The threat, in my opinion, vitiates a good case and raises grave doubts about the *bona fides* of the signatories. Are the Government to yield to cold reason or to the cold steel?

If the Bhandaris have a good case, why do they not rely upon its commanding public sympathy? Let me inform the public that the Ministers are trying their best, in spite of threats, to remove every kind of injustice. In these days of the growing violence of the mind, threats must be regarded as the ordinary lot of Ministers elected under the extensive democratic franchise. They may not be deterred even at the cost of their offices or lives from doing what they hold to be their duty, nor can they afford to be angry and refuse to do justice because, as in the case under consideration, the petition for justice ends by issuing an ugly threat. I have, therefore, pleasure in informing the public that the Ministers are applying themselves to the task of keeping every tapper employed at the very work to which he has been used. Only the tappers have got to help the Ministers to apply the remedy. It consists in the tappers tapping *nira* during the *nira* season and turning it into *gur*. This requires honest care and attention. The pots have to be treated as has been pointed out in these columns. The *nira* need not be drunk. Pure *nira* cannot take the place of toddy which contains a certain percentage of alcohol and which therefore changes in quality. Pure *nira* is food even as sugar is. Toddy, even sweet, is not in the same sense and to the same extent as *nira*. Hence *nira* will be turned into *gur* which can compete with the ordinary *gur* which is often dirty, adulterated, full of grit. Palm *gur* is any day more tasty than sugarcane *gur*. It can be eaten raw whereas sugarcane *gur* being much sweeter does not admit of being eaten raw. And palm *gur*, when it is manufactured under State supervision, will always carry with it the guarantee of being pure. Many sweets can be manufactured out of palm *gur*. But in order to accomplish this great task, whole-hearted co-operation of the Bhandaris is necessary. If they are in earnest, they will help the Government and help themselves. What to do during the off-season will be a question. I have not been able to study the condition under which toddy is drawn. But this is a matter of detail and adjustment.

On the way to Peshawar, 7-7-'39
Harijan, 15-7-'39

37

AN EXPLANATION

To the Editor, the *Harijan*, Poona.

Dear Sir,

My attention has been drawn to the criticism of Mahatma Gandhi on the last para of the memorial presented by the Bhandari Committee to the Hon'ble the Prime Minister of Bombay, which appeared in the issue of the *Harijan* dated 15th July 1939.*

In this connection, I have only to say that the signatories to that memorial acted *bonafide* and they never intended to offer any threat to the Bombay Ministry. The last para of the said memorial was a frank expression of the Bhandari Committee of its apprehensions about the probabilities that might ensue from the enforcement of the prohibition policy under the circumstances then prevailing.

I shall be thankful to you if you will kindly give publicity to this letter at your earliest convenience.

Yours faithfully,
Bombay, 31st July, 1939. S. K. Bole

I gladly publish the foregoing letter and accept the explanation. Without it, the concluding paragraph of the

* See the previous article.

petition could only be interpreted as a threat. Better than the explanation, however, will be the help the Bhandaris could render in the prosecution of the prohibition programme. Let them be true soldiers of the Congress Government and the nation as they were of the East India Company who were foreigners come to exploit the country. If they will heartily assist the Government in their arduous task, they will find that they will also assist themselves in a manner they never otherwise could have done.

Segaon, 7-8-'39
Harijan, 12-8-'39

38

A DANGEROUS GAME

Subhas Babu has played a most dangerous game by mixing up the communal question with such a purely moral reform as prohibition. It is as much the concern of a Muslim or a Parsi or a Christian as of a Hindu to look after his less fortunate countryman who happens to be a labourer and falls a victim to drink. The Bombay property-owners will pay one crore rupees as additional tax not because they are Parsis or Muslims but because they are property-owners. It is altogether misleading to suggest that the tax-payer, himself a non-drinker, will pay the tax for saving the drunkard. He will pay the tax for the education of his children whereas hitherto the drinker has been made by him to pay for that education. The additional tax will be a tardy but very small reparation for the wrong done by moneyed men to the poor. And the poor have no class. They, irrespective of their caste and creed, make by themselves a downtrodden class. Their enforced creed is wretched poverty.

Parsis are philanthropists of the world. Why should they be behindhand in this the greatest philanthropy ? And if theirs is the greatest contribution, it is but in accordance with their best tradition. And they will be thrice blessed. Many of them will be weaned from a trade which corrupts the morals of their countrymen less fortunately placed than they. They will themselves be weaned from the drink habit. However mild it may be for them, I know, from having lived in intimate contact with them, that drink does leave an indelible mark on them. Thirdly, moneyed men amongst them will have paid for the long delayed reform. The cry of minorities is a calumny. It is a Parsi Minister to whose lot has fallen the privilege of introducing prohibition. Dr. Gilder's is a job which brings him no money and it brings him drudgery and loss of a princely medical practice. Another equally disinterested physician is the Sheriff of Bombay. A third learned Parsi is Vice-Chancellor of the University and a fourth businessman is the Mayor of Bombay. I do not know that there has been such a happy conjunction before in the history of Bombay. If the Congressmen and the Congress Ministry of Bombay were communally-minded and were indifferent to the minorities, this unique event would not have taken place.

And I suggest that without the willing co-operation of the Muslim population of Bombay, the movement in Bombay could not have been introduced. I am quite sure that the best Muslim mind in all India is with the Congress in this Bombay project.

Abbottabad, 13-7-'39
Harijan, 22-7-'39

C. UNDER GOVERNMENT OF FREE INDIA

39

TOTAL PROHIBITION

National Provincial Governments are now in full swing in India. Happily on the question of prohibition, there can be no difference of opinion between the Congress and the Muslim League. And if all followed a concerted policy and the States too joined in, India would be dry in no time and earn the blessings of lakhs of homes. To the discredit of the Governments under virtual martial law, Governors and their Advisers had the shamelessness to reverse the policy which had been already adopted in some provinces and misappropriate the revenue which was raised by the provinces in question. Let them now take up prohibition of intoxicating drinks and drugs. Let them, too, not rest content with prohibition legislation. They have to devise methods of educating the drinking public in the harm that drink does and provide them with innocent recreation and health-giving drinks. Every bar or, failing that, a place next door to it should, so far as possible, be utilized as a refreshment and recreation room. If this constructive activity is taken up, it must prove a source of revenue for the State besides prohibition benefiting and reconstructing thousands of ruined homes.

Moreover, toddy-tapping should be replaced by *nira*-tapping for the purpose of converting *nira* into *gur*, much to the advantage of the nation which needs cheap sugar. These columns have shown how in some ways *tad-gur* is preferable to cane-*gur*.

These reflections are suggested by the following paragraph from a circular letter addressed by the Women's Christian Temperance Union (Fyzabad Road, Lucknow) to the Press. From it, I take the following items addressed to the students under the heading "What can youth do ?"

1. Pledge themselves to total abstinence from all intoxicants and habit-forming drugs, which include tobacco. It helps to sign the pledge.

2. Demand a thorough Alcohol and Narcotic Drugs Education, to be a part of the School Curriculum.

3. Demand while under training a part in Social Service, including temperance work, educating the public of the harm done to them through the use of intoxicants.

4. Recommend that in the Scheme for Small Savings Campaign for rural population, total abstinence from all intoxicants be stressed.

5. Ally themselves against the awful waste of precious foodstuffs for liquor in breweries and distilleries to feed the nation.

6. Join up with a temperance society. The W.C.T.U. has been in this struggle for the last 59 years in India. It needs your encouragement and support. Their motto is : "For God, for Home and Every Land."

7. Make use of temperance literature. Rs. 2/- a year will bring to you a 100 leaflets a month in either Hindi or Urdu, also in some other vernaculars to give away. The monthly magazine, the *Indian Temperance News* in English can be placed in any library (not personal) for a rupee a year. If students wish to subscribe to it, it might have the same reduction.

8. Holidays, a good time for this service.

9. As true patriots, to learn the lesson of how much they can give to the country rather than how much they can get out of it for themselves.

Simla, 7-5-'46

Harijan, 19-5-'46

II. DRINK IN RELATION TO PRIVATE EFFORT

A. GENERAL

40

TEMPERANCE

The work in connection with the liquor habit has got to be primarily done by us. The utmost that the Government can do or be made to do in this respect is to cease issuing toddy licences but it can hardly wean the drunkard from his ill habit. That part of the work will still have to be undertaken by private effort..

Young India, 13-9-'28

41

CONSTRUCTIVE PROGRAMME

Not till we pierce the home of the drunkard shall we make any real advance. We must know why he drinks; what we can substitute for it. We must have a census of all the drunkards of India.

Young India, 2-3-'22

42

PROHIBITION

If we are to reach our goal through non-violent effort, we may not leave to the future government the fate of lakhs of men and women who are labouring under the curse of intoxicants and narcotics.

Medical men can make a most effective contribution towards the removal of this evil. They have to discover ways of weaning the drunkard and the opium-addict from the curse.

Women and students have a special opportunity in

advancing this reform. By many acts of loving service they can acquire on addicts a hold which will compel them to listen to the appeal to give up the evil habit.

Congress Committees can open recreation booths where the tired labourer will rest his limbs, get healthy and cheap refreshments, and find suitable games. All this work is fascinating and uplifting. The non-violent approach to Swaraj is a novel approach. In it, old values give place to new. In the violent way such reforms may find no place. Believers in that way, in their impatience and, shall I say, ignorance, put off such things to the day of deliverance. They forget that lasting and healthy deliverance comes from within, i.e. from self-purification. Constructive workers make legal prohibition easy and successful even if they do not pave the way for it.

Constructive Programme—Its Meaning and Place, pp. 10-11, edn. 1941.

43

A STUPENDOUS TASK

Gandhiji who, since the Congress resolved to accept offices, has been burning the candle at both ends, may now be said to be devoting all his waking hours to the problem of prohibition and mass education, and the more he is consulted on these problems the more readily he comes out with fresh ideas and fresh proposals.

"What are the most effective agencies for the creation of a sober India?"

"I have said already that the existing excise force may be used to advantage. Up to now they had no belief in the Government's *bona fides* to achieve prohibition at even a distant date. They now know well enough that the Congress will not rest in peace and will not let others rest in peace until it has achieved prohibition, and they will gladly fall into line with the new policy and programme. But the voluntary agencies will be more effective. There are our professors and teachers, and students of colleges. They may well be called upon to devote a couple of hours each day to the task. They should go to the areas frequented by the drinkers, associate with them, speak to them and reason with them and do peaceful picketing of an educative character. I look to the medical profession to put their heads together to find out why people drink, how they can be weaned from drink, find out effective, wholesome and healthful substitutes of drink. Then there are our sisters. They did great work during the non-co-operation days. They should be organized again to revive the work under better auspices now. Whilst their presence will be a sure deterrent, they will have few difficulties in the way. Before, the police looked indifferently on, and even helped the ruffians in the days gone by. Now, women can count on their help in their holy crusade. Then there are the temperance associations. Most of them have been up to now inert and inactive. We should now ask them to pull themselves together and engage actively in the crusade. We might well have a Prohibition League under which all these agencies may work in a regular and systematic manner. The revenue drawn from excise may rightly be used for the prohibition campaign. That will be no forbidden use of tainted money, but something like turning a channel of foul water into the holy Ganga and making it pure.

" Above all find out the plague spots, concentrate your forces on them. Have meetings of the liquor contractors and liquor dealers, teach them how to turn an honest penny by converting their liquor booths into recreation centres. I have already described how these places may be turned into centres of harmless recreation and even of educative amusement."

It has been suggested that drink is a necessary accompaniment of the factory system, in fact all labour, involving arduous and cheerless toil. Farmers working in the rain or in wet paddy fields, we are told, need something to warm themselves up. The medical friends who sit down to suggest measures to meet all these difficulties and many others have a tough task before them, but it should not be difficult for them to cope with it. Thus I have seen with my own eyes that where liquor is forbidden even among the agricultural labourers, a quarter of a pound of *gur* and an equal amount of onions are considered to be the best possible food during the wet season. There is the *mahura* flower which by itself is a very good energizing food. We should be able to find out how the flower can be made available to the people without exposing them to the temptation of illicit distillation. A correspondent has made suggestions about changes in the conditions and hours of work of the worker in the city and in the village, which are worth consideration :

"In cities (1) there should be limitation of hours of hard work; (2) the barrow drawers' and rikshaw drivers' loads should be limited ; (3) handling of heavy loads should be done more in mornings and evenings ; (4) in summer at least, between 12 and 2 p.m. there should be rest and light labour.

"In villages during harvest time peasants working in the hot periods get easily tired and crave for stimulants. Their working hours should be limited to eight, between two periods, from 5-30 to 10-30 a.m. and 3 to 6 p.m. I hear this system is followed in the Straits Settlements. I have seen in Namakkal people going for harvest in the cool hours of the night. When the paddy is being beaten, they expose themselves to the hot sun. A pandal above their heads in the *kalam* (the place where paddy is beaten off) will be helpful. As the paddy liberates dusty and irritating particles and these settle down on the naked body, the peasants wish to forget the irritation through drink. They should be encouraged to wear shirts.

"As a very good substitute for drink, I suggest the ancient practice of drinking *panagam* be revived. It is made of cold water, jaggery, lime juice and *sabja* seeds. This will give energy and also cool the system. Sour buttermilk may also be suggested."

Harijan, 28-8-'37

B. LIQUOR ADVERTISEMENTS

44

LIQUOR ADVERTISEMENTS

At the Temperance Conference in Lahore one of the resolutions adopted was as follows :

> " This Conference is of opinion, that there is no justification whatever for permitting advertisements and placards of liquors in public places and newspapers, and is strongly of opinion that these solicitations should be immediately prohibited, even if it is considered for any reason that sale of liquor cannot be stopped at once. This Conference appeals to all newspapers having the interest of the people at heart to abstain from publishing such advertisements, whatever the pecuniary sacrifice incurred may be."

It is a matter for sorrow, that in a country like India, where drink is almost universally admitted to be a vice, there are respectable newspapers enough to be found to take advertisements for the sake of spirituous liquors whilst their editorial columns favour total prohibition. I hope, that the resolution of the Conference will move the newspapers concerned to stop taking the offending advertisements. There may be the question of contracts made with advertisers. Since the proprietors of the newspapers concerned have wronged the nation in taking the advertisements, it is not too much to expect them to part with a portion of the ill-gotten profits in paying for such damages as may be necessary for ending contracts before their times.

Young India, 9-1-'30

C. PICKETING

45

PICKETING

Picketing in its nature must be temporary, but it is like what a stimulant is in medicine. Drink is more a disease than a vice. I know crores of men who would gladly leave off drink if they could. I know some who have asked that the temptation might be put away from them. In spite of the temptation having been put away at their instance, I have known them to steal drink. I do not, therefore, think that it was wrong to have removed the temptation. Diseased persons have got to be helped against themselves. If I have a son who is addicted (say) to gambling, and a gambling company imposes itself on me to tempt my boy, I have either violently to knock the company down or to post watches at its offices, in order, if possible, to shame my son into not going there. It is true, that there are other gambling companies some distance from my place. Still I take it, I would be held in the right in having posted a watch at the company's door. I must make it difficult for my son to gamble. If the *Reformer* accepts the doctrine of State prohibition, it must accept the corollary of picketing, so long as the State is a tyranny being perpetrated in the face of public opinion. What, for instance, should the public do, if the State were to build palaces in every street for women of ill fame, and issue to them licences to ply their trade ? Will it not be its duty, unless it destroy these palaces inhabited by vice, to quarantine them and warn the public of the danger of falling an easy prey to the temptation forced on it ? I recognize the necessity of using only men and women of character as pickets and of guarding against violence being offered to those who insist on drinking in the face of public opinion. Picketing is a duty a citizen must discharge, when he is not helped by the State. What is a police patrol, if it is not picketing against thieves ? The police use the gun, when the thief betrays an inclination to break into another's house. A picket uses the pressure of shame, i.e. love, when he warns a weak brother against the dangers of the drink evil.

Young India, 6-7-'21

46

AN INJURED EYE

Attention has been drawn in these columns to the temperance activity in Ahmedabad and its great self-restraint. Dr. Kanuga was so seriously hurt in the eye by an unknown stone thrown that he might have lost it. As it was, he had to be laid up for a few days. He stood his ground in spite of the injury till he was relieved. The other pickets continued at their post. There was no panic. Naturally there was no complaint. The result was electrical. The drinking party was nonplussed. The stonethrowing lost its force for want of reaction. And I understand that, after the incident, there has been no stonethrowing at all. The effect on the visitors to the drink shops has also been equally great. I regard this as one of the best examples of non-violence and its immediate results. Had Dr. Kanuga complained to the police, or his companions retaliated, there would have been a confusion of issues. All kinds of side issues would have been raised, and, as usual, feelings would have run high among parties, and, what is worse, the cause of temperance would have suffered a setback. Dr. Kanuga's bravery, sacrifice and self-restraint have advanced the cause for which he has bled, it has checked any further exhibition of temper on the part of the publicans and their friends and raised the temperance crusade to a very high level.

Young India, 20-4-'21

47

BROKEN HEADS

I understand that two pickets were struck by some ruffians and had their heads broken in Ahmedabad. These brave men now daily appear at their post with bandaged heads. A volunteer was slapped in the presence of a crowd in Bombay, and he stood his ground firmly but did not retaliate. Such instances must multiply, as the effect of picketing is felt by the sellers of spirituous liquors. It is impossible to stop this reform, even though pickets lose their lives in the performance of their duty. The work must continue, so long as there are enough young men and women found ready to take up picketing and so long as they are ready to risk their lives without retaliating. It was because I was aware of the danger, that I appealed to the patriotism of the Moderates with a view to abolishing at a stroke all drink-shops, and thus saving young men and women from injury to limb or life.

Young India, 22-6-'21

48

THE RIGHT OF PICKETING

Where picketing can be practised without violence and ill-will against the liquor-dealer or the drinker, it is a moral duty. That it has advanced the cause of temperance as nothing else has no one can deny. Only the other day at Karamsad the Christian and Hindu Dhedhs gratefully informed me that as a result of picketing they had banished drink from their midst. Bombay has forfeited the right for the time being at any rate because of its wanton and malicious destruction of Parsi liquor shops and its disgraceful behaviour towards Parsis and Christians on the fateful 17th November and the two following days. I hope, however, that wherever picketing is practised, it will be entrusted to men or women of unimpeachable character and carried on in the friendliest spirit. We do not want to make people virtuous by force.

Young India, 22-12-'21

49

RATHER FREE THAN SOBER

Just as I am writing these notes, my assistant puts into my hand a cutting from the *Leader* containing the text of Pandit Gopinath Kunzru's letter describing in the calmest manner possible what befell him and his friend when they were purchasing in Agra brandy from a liquor shop for outward application for a patient. The volunteers would not allow them to take the brandy in spite of all the assurances of *bona fides* given by Pandit Kunzru. This is not only not non-violence but is unadulterated violence. Peaceful picketing does not mean that so long as no physical violence is used, any kind of pressure could be exercised. The volunteers, if they had remained true to their pledge, would have allowed safe passage to Pandit Gopinath and his friend. The picketers' duty is merely to warn drinkers against the vice of drink, not molest them or otherwise prevent them if they will not listen. If we may force temperance upon the people believing it to be good for them, the English administrators and their Indian supporters are certainly performing an analogous operation. They too force the present system on us well believing that it is good for us. If the Swaraj volunteers may, therefore, take such liberties as they have undoubtedly taken in respect of Pandit Gopinath Kunzru, they are seeking not to change the *system* but to change *masters*. I would rather have India free than sober if freedom has to be sold to buy sobriety.

Young India, 23-2-'22

50

HOW TO DO IT

Mr Andrews has endeavoured to answer the query of the Secretary of the Bengal Sevak Sangh as to how to combat the drink evil. His answer is to follow in the footsteps of Pussyfoot Johnson. Whilst he was trying to convert certain English students, he was stoned. The throw resulted ultimately in the loss of one eye. He pardoned the offenders, would not prosecute them and would not take compensation offered by the British Government. That was an instance of non-violence in thought, word and deed. If such non-violence can be ensured here, I would not hesitate to revive the idea of picketing liquor shops again. But we stand discredited. In many places our picketing in 1921 was far from non-violent. The political idea of embarrassing the Government was predominant with us, that of reforming the drunkard was a very secondary consideration. In the struggle of non-co-operation, politics are made to subserve the moral end. If we can reform the drunkard, we reform also the administration and the administrators. Whereas if we suppress the drunkard by force, we may deprive the Government of the liquor or the drug revenue for a time but in the end the suppressed drinker or smoker will raise his head and the Government will raise an increased revenue. Not until we have men and women enough who would carry on picketing for the love of the drunkard even at the risk of their lives, can we dream of reviving picketing.

Young India, 17-4-'24

51

AGAINST PICKETING

A retired Government officer from the South writes:

"I gather from the *Hindu* of Madras that you have published in *Young India* a new code of picketing liquor and foreign cloth shops, and have invited your readers to send you any other rules for picketing they might think of. May I venture to suggest *Punch's* famous advice: 'Don't' in this connection? In your most excellent address to the journalists explaining the terms of the Peace Pact you said among other things that freedom was not worth having if it did not include freedom to err and even to sin, and you pointed out that when Almighty God Himself had given the humblest of His creatures full freedom even to sin, it was unthinkable that any man should dare to deny the same complete freedom to his fellow creatures. May I most respectfully ask you then why you are toiling night and day to prevent people from drinking liquor or wearing foreign cloth if they like to do so? If you would care to follow *Punch,* would you not be more consistent in your words and deeds? Besides there is one very important point that should not be lost sight of. If picketing were to be legalized, or once picketing as advocated by you is recognized as a lawful method, it might be employed in many cases with results that are shuddering to think of. I will mention just one such case. Religious missionaries are now trying to persuade people to be 'converted'. If Christian and Mahommadan or any other preachers were to picket Hindu temples for the purpose of achieving their objects, what would be the condition of India? You might probably lay down a rule in your code, that picketing was not to be employed in any religious connection. But is that not admitting that picketing as a principle has no legs to stand on? Further, besides religion there are several other departments of life in which picketing could be easily employed without deviating in the least from any of the provisions of your code, with results that would be totally embarrassing. I hope you will not fail to bestow your best thought on the matter and be quite sure that in encouraging picketing in any form you are not helping to 'sow the wind'."

The writer is plausible but not convincing. He forgets that picketing is as old as time. It does not need legalizing.

The Settlement * does not legalize that which was illegal before it. Picketing is the right of a reformer which he may not give up without giving up his cause.

The writer has been betrayed into the common error of thinking that because a man has the freedom to err or to sin, any warning against sin would be an unpardonable interference with the freedom. The fact is that individual freedom to sin carries with it the freedom on the part of the public to wean the sinner from his sin and even to legislate against it. 'The wages of sin is death.' No one can sin or err with impunity. What I have protested against and what the world has always resented is the arrogant and unctuous assumption by authority to force people against their will to be 'good' and to claim infallibility about its standard of what is good and what is bad. Peaceful picketing, on the other hand, is a friendly warning against a practice that a reformer thinks to be bad. When it goes beyond that point, and becomes violent, the law steps in and prevents the person from interfering with the human liberty. The writer has pictured the dangers of picketing in certain conditions. He is not even original in his illustrations. Temples have been picketed before now. Only the attempt proved futile and was given up. And there is nothing to prevent any person from renewing such picketing so long as he observes the rule of the game and does not mind public opprobrium. Picketing of drink and drug shops and foreign cloth shops has been possible and largely successful because there is a public feeling against these shops. There is therefore no danger of the Congress having 'sown the wind and reaping the whirlwind!' Picketing of the educative type has come to stay, for it has proved its usefulness.

Young India, 23-4-'31

* Gandhi-Irwin Settlement, 1931.

D. WOMEN TO PICKET

52

APPEAL TO WOMEN

In connection with the temperance movement, Mr Gandhi appeals to the women of Gujarat to help in the campaign. They should visit the liquor shop localities and plead with the liquor-sellers. If they do not succeed with them they should approach the drinkers. They should scrupulously avoid harsh language. " You are our brothers ; our brothers will not drink. In the name of God, give up drinking." This, and this much only, would suffice for their lecture. " I am sure," adds Mr Gandhi, " they will succeed in shaming the drinkers into leaving the shops. And even if they do not, and behave improperly towards them, even if they abuse them, I would ask them to put up with the abuse for the sake of the country."

Young India, 30-3-'21

53

MEN'S PART

We men may not meddle with the women's picketing of liquor and foreign cloth shops. If we do, we are likely to make a hash of it as we did in 1921. We can assist them in a variety of ways. The two classes of picketing have been designed to provide them with a special and exclusive field of activity. We can help by making the acquaintance of liquor and toddy dealers and interviewing them personally and asking them to give up the traffic now that the nation is going through the throes of a new birth. One can help also by showing greater and more delicate respect towards our women. Such general levelling up of the atmosphere will act upon the liquor dealer and also the foreign cloth dealer and buyer and the drinker as neither will then be able to resist the appeal made to the heart by the gentle sex. In my opinion these are virtues in which *women* excel men. *Ahimsa* is pre-eminently such a virtue. Woman exercises it naturally and intuitively when man reaches it through a laborious analytical process. Women left to themselves are likely quicker to reach the goal than if we men were to meddle with their picketing though we may help them with advice and guidance whenever they need them.

Young India, 17-4-'30

54

LIQUOR PICKETING

There is no doubt danger of violence in picketing. Hence my appeal to the sisters of India to take charge of it. If only the educated few will shed their fear and disbelief the other sisters are sure to follow.

Young India, 24-4-'30

55

HOW TO DO THE PICKETING

1. At least ten women are required for picketing a liquor or foreign cloth shop. They must choose a leader from among themselves.

2. They should all first go in a deputation to the dealer and appeal to him to desist from carrying on the traffic and present him with leaflets setting forth facts and figures regarding drink or foreign cloth as the case may be. Needless to say the leaflets should be in the language understood by the dealer.

3. If the dealer refuses to suspend traffic, the volunteers should guard the shop leaving the passage free and make a personal appeal to the would-be purchasers.

4. The volunteers should carry banners or light boards bearing warnings in bold letters against buying foreign cloth or indulging in intoxicating drinks, as the case may be.

5. Volunteers should be as far as possible in uniforms.

6. Volunteers should at frequent intervals sing suitable *bhajans* bearing on the subject.

7. Volunteers should prevent compulsion or interference by men.

8. On no account should vulgarity, abuse, threat or unbecoming language be used.

9. The appeal must always be to the head and the heart, never to fear of force.

10. Men should on no account congregate near the place of picketing nor block the traffic. But they should carry on propaganda generally through the area against foreign cloth and drink. They should help and organize processions of women to parade through the area carrying the message of temperance and *khadi* and the necessity of boycott of drink and foreign cloth.

11. There should be at the back of these picketing units a network of organizations for spreading the message of the *takli* and the *charkha*, and thinking out new leaflets and new lines of propaganda.

12. There should be an absolutely accurate and systematic account of all receipts and expenditure. This should be periodically audited. This again should be done by men under the supervision of women. The whole scheme presupposes on the part of men a genuine respect for women and sincere desire for their rise.

Young India, 24-4-'30

56

CURSE OF DRINK

A sister writes:

> "On going to the village, I was more than grieved to hear of the havoc drink is working among these people. Some of the women were in tears. What can they do? There is not a woman who would not like to banish alcohol for all time from our midst. It is the cause of so much domestic misery, poverty, ruined health and physique. As usual, it is the woman who has to bear the burden of this self-indulgence on the part of man. What can I advise the women to do? It is so hard to face anger and even cruelty. How I wish the leaders in this province would concentrate on the removal of this evil rather than expend time, energy and brain on the injustice of the Communal Award. We are so apt to neglect the things that really matter for such trivialities as would settle themselves if the moral stature of our people were raised. Can't you write an appeal to the people on the question of drink? It is sad to see these people literally going to perdition because of this curse."

My appeal to those who drink will be vain. It must be. They never read *Harijan*. If they do, they do so to scoff. They can have no interest in being informed of the evil of the drink habit. They hug the very evil. But I would like to remind this sister and, through her, all the women of India that, at the time of the Dandi march, the women of India did listen to my advice and made the fight against drink and the plying of the wheel their speciality. Let the writer recall the fact that thousands of women fearlessly surrounded drink-shops and often successfully appealed to the addicts to give up the habit. In the prosecution of their self-imposed mission, they put up with the abuses of the addicts and sometimes even assaults by them. Hundreds went to gaol for the crime of picketing drink-shops. Their zealous work produced a marvellous effect all over the country. But unfortunately with the cessation of Civil Disobedience, and even before the cessation, the work slackened. Into the reasons for the slackening I need not go. But the work still awaits workers. The women's pledge remains unfulfilled. It was not taken for a definite period only. It could not be fulfilled until prohibition was proclaimed throughout India. The women's was the nobler part. Theirs was to bring about prohibition by emptying drink-shops by an appeal to the best in man. Could they have continued the work, their gentleness combined with earnestness would most assuredly have weaned the drunkard from his habit.

But nothing is lost. The women can still organize the campaign. If the wives of those of whom the writer writes are in earnest, they can surely convert their husbands. Women do not know what influence for good they can exert on their husbands. They wield it unconsciously no doubt, but that is not enough. They must have that consciousness and the consciousness will give them the strength and show them the way to deal with their partners. The pity of it is that most wives do not interest themselves in their husbands' doings. They think they have no right to do so. It never occurs to them that it is their duty to become guardians of their husbands' character, as it is the latter's to be guardians of their wives' character. And yet what can be plainer than that husband and wife are equal sharers of each other's virtues and vices ? But who but a woman can effectively awaken the wives to a sense of their power and duty ? This is but a part of the women's movement against drink.

There must be enough women with proper equipment to study the statistics of drink, the causes that induce the habit and the remedies against it. They must learn the lesson from the past and realize that mere appeals to the addicts to give up drink cannot produce lasting effects. The habit has to be regarded as a disease and treated as such. In other words, some women have to become research students and carry on researches in a variety of ways. In every branch of reform, constant study giving one a mastery over one's subject is necessary. Ignorance is at the root of failures, partial or complete, of all reform movements whose merits are admitted. For every project masquerading under the name of reform is not necessarily worthy of being so designated.

Harijan, 24-4-'37

III. DRINK IN RELATION TO COMMUNITIES

A. CHRISTIANS

57

ARE CHRISTIANS AGAINST PROHIBITION ?

Having received protests from Christian correspondents against prohibition, I asked Mahadev Desai to write to a few representative Christian friends to ascertain their views on the question. Here are two answers. Shri P. O. Phillip, Indian Secretary of the National Christian Council of India writes :

> "I am not surprised to hear that a number of Christian friends are writing to you to say that 'the policy of prohibition trenches upon their privilege to drink.' I may not be far wrong in thinking that most of the correspondents who write to you in that strain are Roman Catholics or those brought up in Anglo-Catholic traditions. Roman Catholic Christianity came to India from Latin countries and is even today dominated by Latin culture. People in Latin countries drink the common wine because in olden days it was not safe to drink water. The Roman Catholic missionaries who came to India, though celibates and given to the simple life, carried with them this national habit of theirs, and the people who accepted their religion naturally followed the example of their priests. There is thus no social or religious disapproval among Roman Catholics in India in regard to drinking in moderation as there is among Muslims and higher caste Hindus. Among Protestant Christians, the attitude towards drink is different.
>
> Though Protestant missionaries come to India mostly from Teutonic countries where beer is the common drink and where there is no taboo on the use of wine, they are generally total abstainers and have taught their Indian converts also to be total abstainers. The result is that the use of alcoholic drink even in moderation is looked upon with social and religious disapprobation among Protestant Christian communities.
>
> Among Roman Catholics also, there is awakening to the evils of drink. While the authorities of the Catholic Church may officially maintain that there is nothing wrong

in drinking in moderation, they cannot shut their eyes to the moral and economic ruin that drink is causing among their people. Drinking even in moderation, when once started, has the fatal tendency to become drunkenness in many, especially among the ignorant and backward.

As a Christian Indian, I rejoice that the Congress Ministries have placed prohibition in the very forefront of their programme. In the past few British and American missionaries lent support to the anti-drink campaign of the Congress, under the mistaken notion that it was adopted only to harass the British Government and not from a genuine desire for reform. Unfortunately, Indian Christians also took their cue from the missionaries and generally kept aloof from the movement. But the sincerity of the leaders of the Congress in advocating prohibition is beyond question. Its adoption is going to involve serious loss of revenues for the Governments for which the Congress Ministries are responsible.

The difficulties in the way of introducing prohibition are stupendous. But the difficulties are there only to be overcome by determined and sustained effort. The undoubted public support there is in India for the total abolition of drink — including, I believe, that of the majority of Christian Indians — will enable the Congress Ministries to overcome these difficulties. The poorer classes in the villages, including Christians, need protection more than any other group of people from the temptations of drink now placed before them. Indian villages will have new life and prosperity when drink is abolished. The Christian Indian community along with other communities stands to gain immensely by this measure.

Whatever may be the national habits and traditions of the missionaries from the West in regard to drink, we may trust that their sense of practical wisdom will lead them to adopt a neutral attitude on this question, if they are unable to give active support to the cause of prohibition. But Christian Indians who love India and care for the real welfare of the rural masses cannot but rejoice at the prospect of prohibition in the six Provinces. They should not have any difficulty in whole-heartedly co-operating with their fellow-countrymen in making prohibition a complete success."

And Rev. A. Ralla Ram, General Secretary of the Student Christian Movement of India, Burma and Ceylon, writes:

"I give my full support to the objective of the Congress to bring about complete prohibition in the country and that those who are asking that we should be satisfied with temperance should not be listened to. In my opinion the Europeans who come to this country should fall in with our aspirations, and I am afraid that if we should respect their feelings in this matter, we shall leave a loophole for many others."

As I have said before, it is for Europeans to make the choice. I know how difficult it is for them to give up a habit of a life-time, considered respectable. But if they will fall in with the great national reform, the incentive should prove strong enough to wean them from the habit. Anyway, even if in the end exemption within well-defined limits has to be given, let us hope that they will be graceful enough to taboo alcohol from their parties and banquets. Exemption will be, if there is to be, a concession to a lifelong habit and not to a weakness or to an extravagance.

Harijan, 11-9-'37

58

ROMAN CATHOLICS AND PROHIBITION

Mr F. A. Plair writing from Lahore resents Shri Phillip's remarks which appeared in these columns recently about Roman Catholics, and contends that prohibition has been preached from time immemorial by the Roman Catholic priests. He concludes his letter by saying, "We all Roman Catholics concur in your prohibition movement and join it heartily."

Harijan, 16-10-'37

B. HARIJANS

59

HARIJANS

I have heard Harijans telling me that drink is prescribed for them on occasions of marriage and death. I can tell you, without fear of contradiction, that that is a suggestion of the devil. It is nowhere written in scriptures. I would ask you, brothers and sisters, not to go near the devil. I hope you will take my advice to heart and it will give me great joy when you will be able to say that you have given up drink.

Harijan, 12-1-'34

C. IN HINDUISM AND ISLAM

60

IN HINDUISM AND ISLAM

Liquor, as we say, is an invention of the devil. In Islam it is said that when Satan began to beguile men and women he dangled before them the 'red water'.

Young India, 14-1-'32

D. JEWS

61

INTOXICATING WINES IN JUDAISM

When I saw that a claim was registered, and accepted by Dr Gilder for the use of spirituous liquors on behalf of Jews, I was much disturbed. For my experience of Jews among whom I had many friends in Johannesburg was wholly against the claim made in Bombay. I therefore wrote to my friend Herr H. Kallenbach to send me an authoritative opinion from the Chief Rabbi in Johannesburg. Here is Dr Landau's opinion :

> "I beg to state that the orthodox Jew may use only specially prepared (kasher) wine for the sanctification of the Sabbath or holidays in the Synagogue after Divine Service and at home before meals, and on the two eves of the Passover Festival.
>
> The wine need not be fermented.
>
> I may state that the use of wine is not a law but a tradition which the orthodox Jew cherishes, as it is referred to both in the Talmud and in Jewish Codes of Law."

If the Jews of Bombay accept this opinion as authoritative, they should withdraw their claim and be satisfied with the juice of fresh grapes which I understand is the original meaning of the word wine. It is worthy of note, too, that even this use has the authority, not of the Jewish scriptures but of tradition only.

Harijan, 16-9-'39

E. PARSIS

62

TO THE PARSIS

A temperance wave is passing over India. The people want voluntarily to become teetotallers. Society is fast developing a public opinion that would consider drinking an unpardonable vice. Many Parsis make a living by running liquor shops. Your whole-hearted co-operation can sweep out of existence many of these plague-spots in the Bombay Presidency. The Local Governments almost all over India are making a discreditable attempt to thwart the movement which bids fair to succeed even to the point of destroying the whole of the Abkari revenue. Will you help the Governments or the people ? The Bombay Government has not yet been seized by panic. But I can hardly imagine that it will have the courage and wisdom to sacrifice the drink-revenue. You have to make your immediate choice. I do not know what your scriptures say about drink. I can guess what the Prophet, who separated good from evil and sang the victory of the former over the latter, is likely to have said. But apart from your own religious belief, you have to make up your mind as to whether you will forward the cause of temperance in a whole-hearted manner or whether you will supinely and philosophically watch developments. I shall hope that you, as a practical community of India, will actively and thoroughly associate yourselves with the great temperance movement which bids fair to outshine every such movement in the world.

Young India, 23-3-'21

63

TOO LATE

A Parsi friend, who sends Rs 10 for the Tilak Swaraj Fund, writing from Bombay says, "Your appeal to the Parsis comes too late. The Government of Bombay has already pocketed this time in advance nearly 23 lakhs of rupees, fearing a movement from you. If the Parsis can be assured that no other community would get into their place and that you can eradicate the evil for all time then I assure hearty support from the enlightened Parsi community." If the Government has taken the full annual charge in advance, those who close their shops for the purpose of advancing the cause of temperance must get a refund when better times come. The liquor dealers are obviously not non-co-operators. There is no reason why they should not apply to the Government for a refund. As for the assurance required by the friend, I can only say that no reform has yet been brought about on his conditions. His argument means that no one need be good unless all become good, whereas reformers set the example by standing alone. My appeal to the Parsis is to join this temperance movement whether the others do or not. As a matter of fact, several among the non-Parsis have given up drink traffic.

Young India, 27-2-'21

64

DANGER AHEAD

The liquor-shop picketing has an intimate relation to Parsis. We will have to exercise great forbearance towards our Parsi countrymen. While we cannot stop picketing altogether, we must meet the liquor dealers in conference, understand their difficulties and explain our own. Mr Godrej has earmarked his donation for liquor prohibition and the uplift of the suppressed classes. Let us not, therefore, think that all Parsis are necessarily hostile to the great temperance movement. At the present moment, an outbreak of violence is the most to be feared from the temperance campaign, unless the moderate Ministers take their courage in both hands, refund all auction bids and close liquor-shops. I assure them that the movement can only be regulated, it cannot be checked. The people are bent on ending liquor-shops, and treating as a crime all liquor-selling except as a medicine by chemists. It is a matter that brooks no delay.

Young India, 29-6-'21

65

LIQUOR AND PARSIS

Several Parsi friends seem to be under the apprehension that liquor picketing is to be confined only to Parsi liquor dealers. This is wholly a misconception. Picketing is now going on all over India in a more or less organized fashion. And in the parts other than Gujarat, there are more Hindu dealers than Parsis. Even in Gujarat, the thousands of toddy trees that are being uprooted belong overwhelmingly to Hindus. Toddy booths owned by Hindus are certainly to be picketed on a most extensive scale. Organized picketing, it should be remembered, has only just commenced. In my speeches, I have made a pointed appeal to Parsis because there is an indissoluble bond between them and me and because they are the most advanced and organized community in all India and therefore more readily amenable to reason. They read newspapers. Parsi liquor dealers attend my meetings, whereas Hindu dealers are too ignorant to do so. The latter can only be reached by personal visits made to them in their own booths or homes. Indeed the response I am getting from Parsi friends is quite encouraging, though not yet adequate. It is a Parsi sister — Mithubai Petit — who assisted among others by a Parsi pleader is organizing picketing in the Surat District. Behram Mehta and Dhanjisha Darbari have gone to jail in the same cause. They were ostensibly arrested for breach of salt laws, but I have a suspicion that they were arrested for the possibility of their undoubted influence spreading among liquor dealers. Any way they were engaged in the anti-drink work as much as the salt Satyagraha. It was a matter of joy to me too that some Parsi liquor dealers who came to me the other day went away satisfied to find that I had fully the intention of picketing toddy booths just as much as liquor shops. One complaint was that we were leaving alone the liquor shops in the adjacent Baroda territory. The charge is true. But I am hoping that the Baroda State people will organize the picketing of Baroda canteens. Prohibition is first and foremost a moral reform. The Indian States are as much interested in it as the rest of India. The States' people may take up this reform and ought to do so.

The friends who saw me raised also the question of their living. It is here that the Parsis as a community have to step in to find a solution. Parsi associations can prepare statistics and organize bureaus for the employment of those who would need relief when the only source of their income is gone, as it ought to have long ago. It cannot be a matter of pride that this great community has so many of its members living on an immoral traffic.

Young India, 1-5-'30

66

A PARSI PROTEST

Nearly 175 Parsis have signed the protest condemning the violence used against Congress pickets, including Sjt. Abid Ali on the 10th August last. The signatories to the protest include barristers, doctors, solicitors and professors. I congratulate the signatories on their protest. May I however suggest to them, that mere protest will perhaps produce very little effect on those who were concerned in organizing the hooliganism ? What is really required is personal contact with the liquor dealers, and framing a scheme for finding some other and honourable work for them and creating among the Parsis strong public opinion against the traffic. The argument that these liquor dealers have advanced is that if they gave up the traffic, some others would take it up. I have suggested to them that their abstention will create a public opinion even outside Parsi ranks and will really make it impossible for others to take up the immoral traffic. I have already recited in these columns the example of the Bhandaris in Ratnagiri District who led the way by giving up the traffic which was their hereditary occupation. Many Kolis have done likewise. If therefore the Parsis would carry out the reform, they would not be pioneers but they would be following a good example and making a patriotic contribution towards eradication of a traffic that is doing irreparable harm to the labouring population.

Young India, 24-9-'31

67

PROHIBITION AND PARSIS

I have read long accounts of a great Parsi meeting in Bombay protesting against prohibition in Bombay. I note that Parsi ladies also took part in the meeting. I have also some letters from Parsi friends appealing to me, as the author of prohibition as a chief plank in the Congress programme, to ask the Bombay Ministry to desist from their policy of prohibition.

It is not clear whether the objection is to prohibition as such or to the new taxation. All India knows the intimate connection that subsists between the Parsis and me. It hurts me to think that this race of the greatest philanthropists in the world should ally itself to a campaign against a cause whose basis is purest philanthropy. The hurt is all the greater for the knowledge that even Parsi ladies have allied themselves to the campaign. I see that unworthy threats were used at the meeting and the rights of minorities were pleaded. I can only hope that all the heat shown at the meeting was due to momentary passion, and that the innate philanthropy of the Parsis will assert itself. I venture to suggest that the Parsis will be among the first to benefit by the prohibition policy. It is wrong to suggest that drink has done or is doing no harm to the Parsis. The Parsis will be the gainers for the diversion of Parsi liquor-sellers to some other means of livelihood.

Let me remind the objectors that prohibition does not affect unfermented toddy which is called *nira*. Therefore no Parsi will be deprived of his *nira* which, I admit, is as healthy as sugarcane juice and perhaps cheaper, if a means can be discovered of preventing quick fermentation which *nira* undergoes more than other sweet juices.

The objectors departed from truth when they raised the cry of attack on religion. I have read the carefully drawn prohibition rules which provide for special permits for the use of spirituous liquors for *bona fide* religious rites. The rules also provide for their use for medical purposes. And so far as taxation is concerned, it ill-behoves philanthropists to grumble at taxation for a cause so noble as prohibition which means the welfare of ignorant millions. I hope, therefore, that the nobler element, of which there is so much among the Parsis, will assert itself and help the glorious movement which promises to deliver the labouring population from a curse which is destroying them body and soul.

New Delhi, 4-4-'39

Harijan, 8-4-'39

68

PARSIS AND LIQUOR TRAFFIC

How I wish Parsis will shed their anger and look at the liquor policy of the Congress square in the face. If they have made it a principle to resist by all means at their disposal the Government's undoubted right to refuse to auction or sell liquor licences, there is no argument left to be advanced. It is the assertion of a principle against principle. But I hope they have taken up no such uncompromising attitude. The deputation of licencees and tappers took up no such attitude.

But apart from the question of principle, there are objections raised against the working out of the policy. They are chiefly about

(a) the right to use wines for religious purposes,

(b) the right to have liquor on medical, i.e. health grounds,

(c) racial discrimination,

(d) compensation to those who will be thrown out of employment, i.e. tappers, contractors and liquor dealers, etc.,

(e) the effect of the property tax on charities.

All these are pertinent questions demanding clear answers. Ministers are bound to remove every valid objection that can be advanced against the working out of the policy.

The right to use wines on religious or health grounds has always been recognized by Dr. Gilder.

I understand that in law there will be no racial discrimination. It may appear to be in the administration of the law. No one will be entitled to have the permit for the asking, not even the European, if only so that the law might not be evaded. Every case will be examined on merits. Even Europeans will be expected to respect the liquor policy of the country and, wherever they can, to refrain from asking for permits. The Archbishop of Bombay, in spite of his unconvincing opposition to the closing of liquor shops, has gracefully announced that he and many under him are not going to ask for permits for their personal use. Many Protestant divines, I understand, have already announced similar self-denial. I should not be surprised if many European laymen copy the estimable example of the European divines. Nevertheless there is no doubt that in the administration of the law, there will be more indulgence to Europeans than to those like Parsis for whom India has been a home for centuries. But I have not the shadow of a doubt that every genuine case will be considered with sympathy. May not the Parsis be expected to fall in with the general sentiment, especially when it conduces to the conservation of the social and economic welfare of the labouring classes ? Enlightened Parsis must surely recognize the necessity of checking the drink evil while there is still time.

The points (d) and (e) cannot be dealt with at all satisfactorily without the hearty co-operation of the parties concerned. Thus, so far as the charities are concerned, it is surely up to the trustees of these charities to support their case with facts and figures. Some hardship no doubt there will be. Every tax is a hardship. But I should be surprised if any single charity is seriously affected. After all, the tax calculated to bring in from the city of Bombay about rupees one crore is so widely distributed that no individual or corporation will be hit beyond endurance. But it is for those who contend otherwise to prove their case.

Liquor dealers have to present their case with full detail so as to enable the Government to deal with it. I understand that most owners of stocks of wine have not even furnished the information asked for by the Government. How is the Government to deal with them, if they will sullenly refuse to help the Government to help them? I know that the Government are taxing themselves to meet every case of proved and avoidable hardship. I use the word 'avoidable' purposely. The Taj will certainly be affected, but that is as much as saying that the liquor-shopkeepers will be affected. The Taj is a mighty liquor dealer. The house of Tata is resourceful enough to devise other and better ways of supporting the many charities for which it is so justly famed. I dare say that the charities themselves will bear richer fruit for their being purged of the questionable income from the drink traffic.

Bombay, 4-7-'39

Harijan, 8-7-'39

DRINK, DRUGS AND GAMBLING

DRINK

PART II : *By Others*

EXCISE FOR REVENUE

(*By B.*)

The contention that excise is a necessary source of revenue will not hold water on examination. It betrays a narrow, short-sighted financial policy. We may even say that it is both false and hollow. The excise policy of the Government ignores the fiscal axiom that the patrimony of the State must in no case be impaired. An unsound financial policy must sooner or later impair it. A Government guided by a sound financial policy would try its utmost to prevent the nation from spending its money on objects that undermine both the health and the morals of the people — and liquor and drugs ruin both. It would likewise not only prevent the money from being spent on "unproductive" goods, it would also direct this along "productive" channels. Liquor is certainly an "unproductive" article. The money spent on it gives no return to the consumer; on the contrary it damages his working capacity, causes loss of efficiency, promotes ill-health and disease, encourages other forms of vice, and prevents the money from being utilized to the advantage of the consumer, and hence of the society and the nation. In short, as Mr Micawber would say, it is a 'malignant growth'.

Supposing, however, that the drink evil is abolished, will not the Government be a sufferer to the tune of 17 crores (the present revenue from excise) ? The answer is simple : it cannot ultimately suffer. By abolishing excise, the nation will have on its hands the money it now spends on drink. The Government derives a revenue of 17 crores, but the nation spends at least 50 crores on drink. The nation can either spend the money or save it. If it saves this huge amount annually, the Government will be able to tax the people accordingly. Every economist from Adam Smith to Marshall has laid down that prosperity is based on thrift, and the taxable capacity of the nation is in proportion to its prosperity. Suppose the nation, instead of saving this money, spends it say on cloth. It will mean more growing of cotton, more manufacture of cloth, more employment and higher wages for the labour. Here again the nation will prosper. Why excise fails as a proper means of taxation is — not to speak of the sin of it — because it accelerates the increasing poverty and chronic starvation of the people. As a doctrine, it is fallacious and unsound ; as a policy it is ruinous and immoral. If this evil takes permanent root among the people, the Government will soon learn to its cost, like the man in the fable, that it has killed the goose that laid the golden eggs.

Young India, 1-6-'21

70

THE RIGHT TO DRINK ?

(By C. Rajagopalachari)

The Government of Bengal has gravely enunciated the exploded doctrine of individual liberty as an argument against total prohibition. The right of the individual to commit acts injurious to himself, his family and to society in general is a fiction born of outworn theories of the liberty of the individual which have long since been discarded by progressive nations. It certainly has no place in India ruled by manners, customs and religions which ever place the interests of society above the so-called right of the individual. The whole mischief really arises out of the fact that our European rulers cannot realize the totally different place that liquor occupies in Indian life from that which it does in Western social life. To drink wine, whisky, gin or brandy is not among them the indecent and wrong thing that it is among the lowest of us. People do drink among us, and thanks to the Government policy, there is not a big village but has a licensed toddy shop where Government insists that a minimum quantity of spirituous drink must be kept for sale. But it is among all castes considered wrong to drink. The women will not allow it to be done at home. Every one that drinks tries to do it away from home and unobserved by friends. This is the great difference, which Europeans brought up in a different way from childhood cannot realize. Any talk about the right to drink would raise tumultuous laughter in an Indian audience, whereas it would be gravely discussed by a European gathering.

Young India, 16-12-'26

71

HAS PROHIBITION FAILED ?

(*By C. Rajagopalachari*)

We are constantly told that drink has not gone down in America in spite of prohibition. Deleterious concoctions, it is said, have taken the place of 'good' liquors; secret unrestrained indulgence has replaced moderate public drinking; and the nation is no better for the new laws. One wonders why if prohibition has not succeeded in reducing the consumption of liquor, the liquor interests are so eager to get a repeal. While it may be admitted that drink will offer the utmost resistance before yielding to the laws of prohibition, and that many years of hard persevering work will have to be gone through before full enforcement of prohibition can be expected in a country like America, the very propaganda and the organized efforts of the Anti-prohibitionists are a sufficient proof that prohibition has materially decreased consumption and will one day bring to an end the liquor trade. Any one can get liquor if he likes, say they. And they contradict themselves the next minute and deplore the fact that men are driven to all sorts of shifts to procure some poisonous substitute for 'good' liquor. The argument that laws are ineffective to stop drink is no more sound than an argument that laws cannot altogether stop theft or adultery and therefore, let us repeal the Penal Code.

The talk about impure liquor being indulged in, because 'good' liquor is not available, is again a curious instance of specious exaggeration to serve selfish ends. Such evasions of the law and indulgence in poisons have their own automatic checks. Those men who will take poison because no liquor is given to them may well be left to themselves. We need not stop our attempts at reform because some men will rather die than give up liquor.

Young India, 27-1-'27

72

CONTEMPT FOR LAW

(*By C. Rajagopalachari*)

There cannot be a more disingenuous argument than the oft-repeated plea of the liquor interests that prohibition has bred contempt for law in America and that consequently the interests of the constitution demand a repeal of prohibition. Those very people who want to nullify prohibition and force a repeal of it, organize and encourage disobedience and evasion of the law and shed crocodile tears, about the spirit of lawlessness that has been engendered by the new law. They seek to get reversal of the law by making it impossible to enforce it. Every minority in a democracy can, if they like, put forth such efforts as the defeated *wets* have done in America, and try to make government impossible. In the beginning a mere spirit of adventure may induce some men to disobey and place themselves in the service of the scheming interests that seek to carry their point by sheer lawlessness. But after a time, when vigorous enforcement has proved the futility of such efforts, the misguided victims will realize the error of their allying themselves with interests obviously selfish.

Young India, 3-3-'27

73

CAN WE AFFORD DRINK ?

(*By C. S.*)

The gross revenue from drink and drugs in the Bombay Presidency in 1935-36 was over Rs 3 crores (Rs 3,29,51,000), and the population of the Presidency in that year was about 180 lakhs (17,992,053). This means that the Excise revenue charges come to little less than Rs 2 per head per year. The actual expense incurred on drink and drugs by people in the Presidency is very much more than this. And if it is borne in mind that the population figures also include women and children and that there are whole classes of people who have never known what liquor is, the incidence of expenses is much heavier than is apparent on those who are victims of the vice. And these are the very classes who form the bulk of those who live in " sub-human poverty " and " on the margin of subsistence " and who hardly know what a full meal is. What a terrible financial drain this means on the resources of the nation, not to speak of the physical and moral degradation that it necessarily involves !

Harijan, 12-6-'37

PROHIBITION LARGELY A CITY PROBLEM

(*By M. D.*)

The following figures taken from the Bombay Excise Administration Report for 1935-36 are eloquent proof of the fact that the prohibition problem is very largely a city problem :

1.	The total consumption of country liquor is	10,40,157	gallons
2.	Consumption in urban area of towns with a population of 10,000 and above is ..	5,76,710	„
3.	Total urban population of the Presidency is	33,41,301	„
	Drink per capita in the urban area	1/6th	„
4.	Out of this urban population Bombay alone consumes ..	2,86,249	„
	i.e. nearly 2/7 of the total consumption or per capita ..	1/4th	„
5.	Rural population is	1,46,50,752	„
	Total consumption	4,63,447	„
	i.e. per capita	1/32	„
6.	Total receipts from country liquor in Bombay Presidency	Rs	1,58,06,401
	Bombay alone pays	„	58,28,742
	Other 32 cities with population above 20,000 pay	„	46,03,412
	Receipts from rural area including towns below 20,000 ..	„	53,74,247
7.	Total receipts from fermented liquor	„	71,15,064
	Bombay pays more than one-fourth	„	18,03,226

With the co-operation of captains of industry the problem which is largely urban can be very easily solved. For mill-owners and factory-owners to start recreation clubs and prohibition restaurants would be a paying proposition, apart from the improvement in the efficiency of labour; and with the help of volunteers and voluntary organizations prohibition in the urban areas could be achieved within less than 3 years. Once the urban problem is solved, the solution of the rural problem, which is not even half so serious, will follow as a matter of course.

Harijan, 11-9-'37

75

THE SOCIAL SIDE OF PROHIBITION

(*By John Barnabas*)

However greatly we may hate drink and endeavour to end it, we may legitimately sympathize with the drinker and try to understand his problems. Any scheme of prohibition which disregards the social side of the problem will harm the individual in the very attempt to help him.

The Need for Drink

Various circumstances give rise to different human needs. While condemning drink wholesale, we must recognize the service it renders to a section of society. The average man is not a wilful drinker. He drinks owing to some external circumstances. In India the toddy shop may well be called 'The Poor Man's Club'. The well-to-do folks have Willingdon Clubs and Gymkhanas of diverse description, to fulfil their instinct of sociability, and to give them recreation even when they do not need it. So does the poor man have the toddy shop for the same purpose. There he finds relaxation after a long day in the dust and roar of the factory such as the crowded and slouchy rooms he calls home will not furnish. Here he can escape the crying children and get the companionship of men interested in the same things in which he is interested. The toddy shop is a democratic institution, open freely to everyone, disregarding caste and creed. For, when you reach there, all are pruned to a common level from where you rise above human sentiments into an etherial state of existence!! Therefore it is that efforts at prohibition are resented as an attack on the poor by the more well-to-do ! ! Thus the toddy shop appeals to a fundamental social instinct — sociability.

While the rich man rolls in wealth and indulges in pleasure, the poor man is bathed in sorrow, worries, poverty and the dread of a monotonous existence. But when he drinks he forgets all that, at least temporarily. However short-lived the pleasure may be, it is a legitimate excuse for drink. In fact to him alcohol is a sort of psychic Aladdin's lamp which he uses to alter his mentality.

His daily work confronts him with many failures and disappointments. Hence he takes to drink which serves as a compensation for failure to derive satisfaction from his work and the ordinary routine of life. Unable to face the uphills of life with his limited resources, he attempts to find shelter from them in drink. It is an escape from reality. He drinks to forget and thereby increases that which he would forget. He binds himself in a vicious circle. To some it offers a " solace to the shame and feelings of inferiority ". He imagines drink to be a " psychic cure-all ". Normal intoxication is not what he is after. There he searches and finds " the exciting phase and the relaxing phase ". It gives him a satisfaction which strengthens him for the next day's drudge.

The need for drink is not only psychic. It is physical also. The industrial labourer who is subject to a monotonous work for six to eight hours, in the din of roaring machines, is bound to suffer a nervous breakdown if there is no stimulant to prevent it. However short-lived the joy may be, drink gives him a new experience of freedom of movement, proves a stimulant to his nervous condition at dusk, and sends his worries and consciousness of poverty to his subconscious existence, which would otherwise wreck him physically and mentally when he is free to think of them after being relieved from work in the evening.

Figures have their own meaning. For want of adequate Indian figures I produce some American. Human nature being the same all over, they may well interpret Indian facts as well. 246 patients in New York were asked, " Why did you begin to drink ? " This was the result : Sociability 52.5 per cent : Trouble 13 per cent : Medical use 9.3 per cent : Occupation 7 per cent : Taught by elders 7 per cent : Out of work 5 per cent : Unknown 5 per cent : To be thought sporty 1.2 per cent.

The Evils of Drink

Generally speaking, the chronic alcoholic becomes indifferent to responsibilities, loses ambition, and his affection wanes. " Although he may be a danger to society he generally manages to escape the lunatic asylum."

Many researches go to show that it is the mentally defective, the feeble-minded that is the easier prey to drink. Mental deficiency causes drink, and drink in its turn causes mental deficiency. It is a vicious circle. For, the strong-willed adult individual has too many other interests, other calls on his attention and other opportunities for his relaxation and self-realization, to surrender so easily to the lotus-like charm of habit-forming drugs. Dr. Anderson's studies of 100 habitual drinkers showed that 37 were feeble-minded, 7 insane, 7 epileptic, and 32 of innate psychopathic constitution. Barrington found in England the relation between mental defect and alcoholism to be .70 to .80.

The evil does not stop with the individual. It trickles down to his children, causes family instability and wrecks his very economic existence. The children are bound to suffer either owing to germinal impairment and foetal injury or to improper care during early childhood and infancy. They are notoriously the victims of neglect and abuse. It was found in Chicago's Juvenile Court that the delinquency of 75 per cent that came to the court could well be traced to the neglect and drunkenness of parents, rather than misfortune. It was also seen that while the poverty of 13 of them was owing to immorality of the mother, that of 160 was due to drunkenness of the father, 92 to that of the mother, and 63 to that of both.

Not only do the children suffer but the whole fabric of family life is endangered. Toddy causes poverty : Poverty causes crime : Crime causes the home to break. From 1887 to 1906 there were 184,568 divorces in the U.S.A. due to intemperance of husband or wife. According to the Census Bureau of U.S.A. one divorce in every five had intemperance as a cause. It is the opinion of many Judges dealing in Domestic Relations that roughly 45 per cent of cases they dealt with were owing to drink, while no other one cause furnished over 14 per cent.

Those who are at present opposed to prohibition do not seem to realize the sex excesses drink leads one to. Sex excesses increase venereal diseases. The loss to national wealth in the form of ill-health, loss of vitality, and loss of productive labour need better be imagined than figured out.

A country like India which prides itself on morality will do well to realize the mighty contribution of drink to immorality. According to the 1909 Report of the Inspector under the Inebriate Acts in Great Britain, on 865 immoral women in Britain reformatories, 40 per cent of the immorality was found to be solely due to drink. Dr. Sanger of Blackwell's Island found that out of 2,000 fallen women 82.5 per cent were addicted to drink, 46.5 per cent had drinking mothers; and 61.5 per cent had drinking fathers. Drink finds its greatest patron in commercial prostitution.

Considering the poverty of India, the money expended is ruinous both to the industrial labourer in the city and to the peasant in the village. The latest Abkari reports point out that the average expenditure on drink in the Frontier Province is Re 0-3-8 and in Bombay Presidency it is Rs 2-5-1, and in the rest of the Provinces it is somewhere between the two. According to the Report of the Whitley Commission, the average expenditure of the worker on intoxicants is Re 1-7-5 in Sholapur out of an income of Rs 37-13-11; and in Ahmedabad Re 1-11-6 out of an income of Rs 39-5-8. *The Bombay Labour Gazette* in June 1932 points out that out of 2,473 labour families 71.6 per cent spent money on drink. Out of 601 that had no families, 91.1 per cent spent money on drink. Prof. Gulshan Rai of Punjab says, "A bottle of country liquor, even if it costs six or eight annas, which I believe is a very low price, if bought too often must make a considerable inroad into the daily wages of the poor wage earner....An expenditure of one-third or one-half of the income on intoxicants is economically ruinous." Dr. M. H. Mann pointed out in 1928 that a good many of the peasants in Surat District lost their lands owing to drink and that indebtedness had increased because of drink. So do the Konkan Co-operative Enquiry Committee and the Industrial Disputes Committee say by their figures. Yet Dr. Colaco says in the Assembly, "Toddy is good. It is like orange juice. So please do not close excise shops."

The Substitute for Drink

One cannot help thanking the Congress for launching on a programme of prohibition when he sees these mighty evils of drink. Prohibition there must be: but it must be an intelligent one. I have endeavoured in the beginning to point out the need for drink, the urge for drink in India. If prohibition is to be successful, you must cater otherwise to these needs which drink is now catering to. Some have not realized the difference between the American social conditions and those of India, and hence they warn us against prohibition on the basis of America's failure. American society prides in "lordly drinking". But India shuns a drunkard. There is the basic emotional antagonism against drink in India. Therefore, if external circumstantial causes are met with, prohibition is bound to succeed. While Prof. Gulshan Rai advises State ownership of toddy shops and Sir Choksy advocates the cultivation of palms to mitigate the dangers of immediate prohibition, I venture to demand for adequate substitutes in the form of recreational facilities to aid the habitual drinker.

The negative and destructive method employed in social reform movements should be accompanied or followed by positive and constructive ones. The State has to find some broad, national and practical methods of counterbalancing the various motives that lead men to patronize the toddy shop. The fight against drink should carefully guard against any plan that deprives men of their opportunities to express their feelings of sociability. For drink has capitalized man's love for friends and yearning for social intercourse.

Substitutes Suggested

(1) Every mill should be immediately required (by the State) to have social welfare activities on as wide a scale as practicable, supervised by a trained social worker.

There they should provide for, (a) cheap and healthy refreshment rooms, (b) reading and entertainment rooms, (c) well-organized playgrounds and sports clubs, and (d) adequate separate arrangements for women.

(2) The Municipality should at once increase the number of parks and playgrounds in the more congested areas, wherever the slightest room is available. These should be of two kinds: (a) those near the mill areas, and (b) those in and around vice areas. Both these should provide healthy entertainment till about nine in the night. Much of its success will depend upon the kind of leadership available.

(3) Every congested vice area should have a Social Settlement.

(4) Some prohibition pictures should be worked up and special, if not benefit, shows should be arranged for the labourers on special days.

(5) A system of moving picture shows in the village is very essential.

(6) An extensive use of radios may well occupy the villager in the evening and it may be of great educative value.

(7) Through the help of trained athletic directors and social workers, indigenous games should be encouraged. Non-equipment games are the most adequate for the villages. These same may help in the revival or encouragement of the old folk-songs, village dramas and *tamashas* which may well occupy the idle hours of the villager.

These are merely a few suggestions which may be put into effect immediately. I do not fail to recognize the economic and administrative difficulties the Provinces will have to face, especially in view of the reduced revenue. But no progress is possible without strenuous efforts to surmount obstacles. The public can suggest what is best for society. It is left to the Finance Minister and the administrative authorities to find the money and men to work out these and such other suggestions.

Prohibition we do need. But prohibition without adequate substitutes will increase social evils and social pathology rather than eliminate them. Keep the man in the street occupied with something good, useful and productive. If no provision is made to occupy the time and energy saved by prohibition, an empty mind may well turn out to be the Devil's workshop.

(This excellent article should be studied by every Excise Minister who would make his prohibition policy a success. Every liquor shop should be turned into a refreshment club. The money is there : the excise revenue during the transition period. — M. K. G.)

Harijan, 18-9-'37

76

THE MODERATE DRINKER

(*By M. D.*)

Among the handful of opponents to the Prohibition Bill in the Madras Legislative Council, the leader was Sir K. V. Reddi Nayudu who spoke on behalf of the moderate drinker. He said : "Drunkenness had to be stopped as highhandedly as could be conceived of. But the mere drinking of a glass of liquor before meals should not be restrained with the rigour that was to be found in the Bill." How fallacious and self-deceptive this argument is was very ably pointed out by the Excise Committee appointed by the Government of Bombay in 1922-23 : "Drunkenness is not a well-defined special or specific effect of alcohol. No clear, terse or accurate definition of drunkenness can be given. It is only a conventional name for a certain conventional degree of alcoholic narcosis ; the word cannot be used with precision or scientific accuracy. Drunkenness differs in degree, not at all in nature, from both the slighter effects of alcohol and from the graver and dangerous degrees of the 'dead drunk' stage. The influence of alcohol upon the nervous system is from first to last narcotic, and the degree of narcosis depends upon the amount of alcohol circulating in the blood and the area of the nerve centres narcotized by it. There is therefore really nothing like a moderate use of alcohol, and even if there is something like moderation in it, it is this moderate use of it and the drinking customs which are the spring of all the mischief....Scientific investigations have shown that the difference physiologically between drinking smaller or larger doses of the alcoholic beverages is one of degree and not of kind. There can, therefore, be no true moderation. It has not yet been clearly recognized that the deleterious effects of alcohol on the body are quite equalled by the deleterious effects on the reasoning faculties and on the character. There is very reliable scientific evidence to show that alcohol, even in small doses, tends to paralyse the higher brain centres."

As for the "drinking of a glass of liquor before meals", the Committee cite the emphatic testimony of Dr. Norman Kerr, President of the Society for the Study of Inebriety:

> "I have no hesitation in making the deliberate statement from my own professional experience that more persons have their lives cut short prematurely by latent chronic alcoholic poisoning, produced by regular alcohol taking in so-called 'moderation' long persisted in than by unmistakable drunkenness. As I publicly stated, nearly half a century ago my observation is that apart from the moral and religious aspect of indulgence, the man or woman who gets drunk for a couple of days once a month, and is during the remainder of the period an abstainer, lives longer on the whole than one who never gets drunk, but who drinks (moderately, respectably, circumspectly if you will), day in and day out, a steady allowance of a few ounces of an average alcoholic intoxicant."

This last emphatic utterance will not, I hope, be taken to be a plea for drunkenness. The point is that the so-called 'moderate' drinker deludes himself into calling himself an abstainer and cutting short his life by slow degrees. The drunken man does not confine his drunkenness to only a couple of days a month and then remains an abstainer for the rest of the month! The one ruins himself by self-delusion. The other deliberately or recklessly ruins himself. Toddy ruins the agriculturist materially and morally both. "Even the salt tax, much as I object to it," said Gopal Krishna Gokhale, "was more capable of being defended than the excise revenue, for in the latter case so much money was taken out of the pockets of the poor and so much misery was added into the bargain."

Harijan, 9-10-'37

A NOTE ON PROHIBITION

(*By a Medical Friend*)

The country is now definitely committed to a policy of prohibition. Therefore the only question that now arises is how best to achieve the desired object. World experience on the subject has a lot to tell us. This experience must be studied in relation to the special conditions which exist in India, the extent of the habit, the national inefficiency it causes, and the classes it affects most. On the basis of this study steps should be devised to help the classes most seriously affected.

The problem of prohibition is such a difficult one that any plan of bringing it into effect must be very carefully considered and only those steps adopted which in advance offer a hope of success. Moreover this is the first constructive effort on the part of the Congress Ministry on a fairly large scale. On its success will, therefore, depend the reputation of the Ministry not only in this country but also abroad, and on its success will also depend the hold of Congress on the people.

World Experience

The types of prohibition tried so far may be roughly divided into three main groups:

1. *Total Prohibition*: The American experiment was of this nature. Total prohibition was enacted and an attempt made to enforce it by the employment of preventive services at a great cost. After 12 years' trial, the thing proved a disastrous failure. The reason seems to have been that the problem was considered purely from a moral and religious point of view and was not treated as a social evil that it is. The result was that not only the State lost huge revenues, but it actually spent additional millions in the attempt to enforce the law. This in no way reduced the actual consumption of alcohol. The only result this experiment seems to have achieved was a very wide-spread disrespect for and breach of the laws of the country. This experiment showed how prohibition should not be enforced.

2. *Taking Profit out of the Drink Trade*: Under this system no private individuals are allowed to manufacture or sell alcohol in any form for human consumption. All public bars, restaurants, hotels, etc., are prohibited from selling alcohol. No advertisements are allowed to be published. The State assumes the monopoly, and alcohol is sold from Government stores at a price which does not encourage "boot-legging". The smallest possible number of stores are maintained by the State and alcoholic drinks are sold from these stores in unopened packages in limited amounts to individuals. The alcohol so brought cannot be consumed on the premises of the stores.

This system has these advantages: Since there is no profit to be made, no one is interested in stimulating the sales. Also because alcoholic drinks are sold at reasonable prices, no boot-legging is stimulated. The total number of stores being small, the effort required to procure supplies for personal use keeps the total consumption low. Above all since no bars or other public places sell alcohol, no public drinking or social treating is encouraged. The State checks the habit and does not sacrifice the revenues entirely. And what is still more important, it does not spend very much on maintaining extensive preventive services and does not in any way encourage law-breaking. The system has been successfully worked in Canada, Sweden and a few other European countries.

(3) *Reducing the number of hours during which alcohol can be sold in public places*: That this regulation does to a certain extent reduce the total consumption is shown by the English example.

The Indian Problem

On the whole the Indian problem is less intricate than the problem in Europe. For practical purposes, all that requires to be done is to keep the temptation of drink out of the way of the industrial workers, peasants and possibly lower middle classes. The other classes do not use alcohol much, and if they do they do not economically damage themselves thereby.

Principles Which Should Guide a Prohibition Policy in India

The most important thing, then, is to consider the question of drink from a purely objective social point of view and not from any moral or religious aspect. The moral or the religious aspect of the problem may be very important, but moral and religious ideas cannot be enforced by legal enactment, they cannot but be left to personal enlightenment. But the social and economic welfare of a people can be achieved by laws. In a country in which spirituality is so much talked about, this distinction must be clearly understood. If the moral issues are mixed up with the social aspects of the question, a great confusion and ultimate frustration of the effort is sure to ensue.

The second point is the question of loss of revenue. Prohibition cannot be enforced without some loss of revenue ; but the loss incurred should be the minimum possible, consistent with the main object in view. The total revenues of the provinces are so meagre that they can ill afford to spare a large part of them, much less can they afford the necessary expense for preventive services to enforce total prohibition. The prohibition policy, therefore, must be enforced gradually and Excise revenue given up as other sources are tapped. No commitment should be made as to the number of years in which the policy would be fully enforced.

Thirdly, it is still more important that in addition to the loss of revenue no excessive expenditure should be incurred on preventive services to enforce prohibition. To lose 2 or 3 crores of rupees of revenue from excise may be worth while, but to sink an additional large amount on enforcing prohibition would be very undesirable ; the more so as the nation-building activities are already starved for want of funds. Further such expenditure on preventive services can never bring about prohibition, that is the world experience. Therefore it is essential that only such policies should be adopted as do not require the use of large preventive services to enforce them.

Fourthly, there is only one evil greater than spending money on preventive services, and that is to set neighbours to spy on each other with a view to enforce prohibition. This should never be countenanced. To exploit public fervour for this purpose in the name of patriotism, religion, morality or loyalty to Congress would be a great tragedy. Such a step would embitter social relations of the people and give rise to the worst of heresy hunts. It would disrupt the nation with discord, while it is the primary duty of a good Government to promote social harmony. If spying cannot be avoided, let it be done by a body of Government servants or specially enrolled volunteers who would discharge this function in their official capacity.

Public fervour may, of course, be utilized to carry on an educational propaganda. But such a propaganda must be free of unnecessary social coercion. It should be maintained on a purely rational basis.

Fifthly, any gradual stages of prohibition decided upon from time to time should be enforced at one time over the whole province or even all the provinces which are willing to collaborate. To pick out small areas for special enforcement of prohibition is not likely to bear fruit. It is sure to enmesh Government in tremendous difficulties. It will entail enormous expenditure for such enforcement, and is sure to cause unnecessary annoyance to the public through search of their baggage after short journeys and will unduly hamper movements of merchandise.

Actual Steps

1. The most essential and urgent step to decide upon would be to gradually close down public bars or shops where alcohol is served in small or large quantities for consumption on the premises.

2. No private interests should be allowed to manufacture alcoholic drinks specially distilled or hard drinks. But since no country can get along without the use of distilled alcohol for industrial, technical, medicinal or other scientific purpose, the manufacture of alcohol should be undertaken by the State itself or it should be entrusted to private firms under licence.

3. Foreign imported alcoholic drinks should be allowed to be sold in their original unopened packages. The best way, of course, would be for the State to undertake import

and sale of these drinks. But such a policy may not appeal to the Congress. It would, therefore, be necessary to allow private firms to sell them as at present. Only the total number of shops selling such drinks may be reduced.

Such a policy would do away with the need of any extensive preventive service. Those who need alcohol badly would be able to get it. But having got it they would have to consume it in their own homes. The worker and the peasant would not be exposed to the temptation as there will be no bars or shops retailing open drinks. Further the imported drinks are so expensive that they will be out of the reach of the working classes, whom it is especially desired to help in the matter.

4. Permission to sell imported alcoholic drinks will lessen to some extent the loss in revenue caused by closing bars, etc., as suggested under 1. The province should bring in a sort of sales tax on an *ad valorem* basis on alcoholic drinks sold in original packages. This tax should be made as heavy as the sales would bear. People who usually consume these drinks can afford to pay more for them, and also by increasing the price of alcohol, it will be kept out of the reach of the classes which it is specially desired to keep.

5. To begin with, hotels and restaurants, where meals —real meals —are served, should be allowed to serve imported drinks to those who order meals. But these places should be heavily taxed for this privilege. If and when more experience has been gained of the results of such a policy, the question of preventing even such places from selling alcohol may be considered.

6. *Toddy*: The question of toddy should be very carefully considered. In a number of provinces palm trees grow easily and yield an excellent drink. The juice when fresh is absolutely non-alcoholic and very pleasant. People like it, and it undoubtedly has some nutritive value. Because the juice can be easily fermented to yield a mild alcoholic drink and because it is sold at present largely in a fermented form, it would be no justification for destroying a natural product and a very extensive industry. The toddy juice can be actually used as a valuable agent to bring about prohibition.

The greatest evil of the present sales of toddy is not that it is sold in a fermented alcoholic form, but that it is sold in an adulterated form. I am informed that it is practically impossible in a city like Bombay to purchase unadulterated toddy. Cheap habit-forming drugs are added to this drink.

It is quite easy to collect toddy from trees in an unfermented form. At present the same pots are used over and over again, without cleaning them in between each collection, with the definite object of facilitating fermentation. Yeast grows in them and brings about quick fermentation. If pots are scalded with boiling water in between the collections, absolutely fresh juice could be obtained. Further, if a preservative like sodium benzoate is added in the strength of 0.2 per cent immediately after toddy juice is collected, it would not ferment for days. There is an extensive choice of such preservatives. Experiments could be conducted to choose the best for our purpose. Toddy then can be collected in an unfermented form and can be prevented from fermenting.

The next step is to cut the private profit motive out of the sales of toddy. This will see to it that no adulteration takes place. It would therefore be essential for the State to take over either on hire or purchase at a strictly reasonable price all toddy-yielding trees, and have them tapped by its own agents. An efficient Government agency for the purpose could be organized. Under such arrangements, the juice would be properly collected, would be taken to Government depots and preservatives added which would render subsequent fermentation impossible. From the depots toddy could be sent out, as milk is sent out of dairies, either in open containers for immediate sale in small quantities to consumers or in bottles. The State could run its own bars for the sale of fresh toddy, or the sale could be arranged through provision of milk shops on a commission basis.

Such an arrangement would not disturb an extensive industry, would not throw out of employment a large number of people, and above all, provide a healthy pleasant drink to those who desire it, and by so doing keep them off alcohol drink, and, what is also important, the industry would yield good revenue.

(This is a valuable contribution to the discussion on prohibition. Whilst there are things which cannot be accepted, there are suggestions which are worthy of consideration. The writer adopts the slippery road of gradualness for the sake of revenue. That way lies utter failure. But the suggestion about State monopoly of manufacture and sale of intoxicants and about unfermented toddy is perfectly sound. — M. K. G.)

Harijan, 13-11-'37

78

ADVANCE PROHIBITION

(*By M. D.*)

All the Congress Governments are committed to a policy of complete prohibition, and all have begun the experiment in right earnest and in their own way according to the circumstances in their respective provinces. The Madras experiment has been on since October 1st, 1937, and it is being conducted with the vigilant care and the thorough-going way which characterize everything that is associated with the name of the Madras Prime Minister. The enforcement was in the hands of the police working under the District Magistrate and the District Superintendent of Police assisted by a Prohibition Officer and a Special Development Officer. The results of the experiment achieved so far have been noted in detail in his latest report by the Collector, Mr A. F. W. Dixon, who was in no way pre-possessed in favour of the experiment. In his long report of sixteen foolscap typed sheets, he has in no way overdrawn the picture. He notes the large increase in the number of palmyra trees tapped for sweet toddy, as also the evident risk of their being tapped for fermented toddy if there was not the necessary vigilance; he also notes a few cases of smuggling of *ganja* and opium, and says that, without non-official help, it will not be possible to put a stop to smuggling; he also says that illicit distillation is being kept under control and appears to be going on only on a small scale and in a very secretive manner; he notes to some extent a tendency to drink methylated spirit and asks the District Medical Officer to write a Tamil leaflet describing the deadly effects of drinking the spirit ; also an increase in gambling arising out of the attempt by former drinkers to relieve the boredom of the evening hours ; but notes on the whole that "as month succeeds month without general signs of a deterioration in the situation, the chances of ultimate success become rosier."

This much regarding the success of the actual working of prohibition. When he comes to the effect of prohibition on the lives of the people, he notices a definite improvement all round and summarizes the large mass of information received from various resources and also his own personal impressions in about six sheets. Suffice it to say here that this is the deliberate conclusion he has arrived at as a result of his own impressions on observations :

> "Viewing generally the effect of prohibition on the lives of the people, I am convinced, after 3 months' experience, that prohibition is proving a great boon to the poorer classes in the District. Leading as they do a hand-to-mouth existence, they simply cannot afford the expensive luxury of drink which used to reduce the small earnings of the labouring classes to a miserable pittance, quite insufficient for the proper maintenance of a family. Drink brought misery into the homes of many thousands of the poorer classes in this District, misery in the shape of domestic unhappiness, insufficiency of food and crushing debt. Already in thousands of homes in this District conditions have changed to a remarkable extent. Domestic brawls have ceased, a sufficiency of food is available, and the grip of money-lender has relaxed. This has happened within a short space of four months. If the Act continues to be enforced not less effectively than it is now, I anticipate a great and permanent improvement in the material well-being of the peasants and labourers of this District."

Let us see how much these good results have cost. Said C. R. in his Budget Speech : "The net cost of prohibition for the last six months of the financial year 1937-38 will amount to Rs 13,19,000 made up of Rs 13 lakhs loss of Excise Revenue and Rs 51,000 cost of additional police and special officers, offset by a saving of Rs 32,000 on the excise staff previously employed in the District." Who will say that the moral and material results do not far outweigh this cost ? Apart from individual cases here is a case of the moral effect of prohibition as applied to a mill area affecting 2,000 workers. Whereas these workers were irregular and inefficient before prohibition and night brawls were a regular feature of the area, the workers have now become regular and more reliable, the brawls have now ceased, machines are better looked after, "production increased and expendiure decreased. The outturn has actually doubled. Women were sickly, dirty and clad in rags. Now every woman has two or three *saris*, most of them have petticoats, and 50 per cent wash daily. Their financial position has improved, they have redeemed their jewels, which they mortgaged due to extravagance. Children are better clad and cleaner. Dwelling houses have improved and lights have been introduced into houses which were formerly unlit."

The United Provinces Government have also set about the task in right earnest and their experiment, like the Madras one, has several features which might be copied in other provinces. The main features of the Madras experiment may be summarized below :

(1) Encouragement of tapping for sweet toddy and converting it into *gur*.

(2) Enforcement of the whole policy through the Police staff, and not the Excise staff.

(3) Employment of non-official agencies, like Taluka Prohibition Committees and Village Committees.

(4) Propaganda and provision on counter-attractions.

To these may be added the principal features of the experiment in the United Provinces :

(1) State-managed shops in four selected districts where prohibition has not been introduced, ensuring the strict observance of hours of sale and providing against deleterious adulteration. No consumption at premises.

(2) Reduction of the number of shops in non-prohibition districts by 25 per cent.

(3) Raising of the retail price of opium and *charas* and making it impossible for the vendor to sell these drugs at any price below maximum.

As regards the first feature of the Madras experiment, it may be noted that the fixation of a certain quantity of lime checks the starting of fermentation. In Salem, 10 co-operative societies of toddy-tappers have been registered, and 9 of these which have started work have sold through the Salem Sale Society 19,865 lbs. of *gur* for Rs 975-14-0. It is expected that 50 or 60 more societies will be formed, and that 75 per cent of the old tappers will be engaged in sweet toddy tapping. This experiment deserves to be copied in all parts where there are palm and palmyra trees which are being tapped today for toddy.

Too great an emphasis cannot be placed on the Excise Ministers of different provinces getting into touch with one another, comparing notes and trying in their own provinces the measures that have been tried with success in other provinces.

Harijan, 12-3-'38

DRINK, DRUGS AND GAMBLING

DRUGS

PART I: *By Gandhiji*

79

OPIUM POLICY OF THE GOVERNMENT

Mr C. F. Andrews has shown me a paragraph in his writings in *Young India* regarding the opium policy of the Government of India. In that paragraph he quotes Mr Campbell, the Government representative at the Geneva Conference held in May 1923. Mr Campbell is reported to have stated that "from the beginning India had handled the opium question with perfect honesty of purpose, and not even its most ardent opponents including Mr Gandhi had made any reproach in that respect." The statement Mr Andrews has shown me was written whilst I was a prisoner in the Yeravda jail. Mr Andrews tells me that, knowing my views in the matter of opium, he did not hesitate to contradict Mr Campbell's charge against me, but in view of the importance of the matter he wants me to state my position clearly regarding the opium policy of the Government of India. I do so gladly.

I confess that my study of the opium question is very cursory, but the campaign against drink that was taken up in 1921 with such great enthusiasm and even fierceness, was a campaign not merely against the drink curse but against all intoxicating drugs. It is true that opium was not specifically mentioned, nor were opium dens picketed, except perhaps in Assam ; but those who know anything of the history of the anti-drink campaign, know that sustained agitation was led against all manner of intoxicants not excluding even tea. During my travels in Assam Mr Phookan, the Assam non-co-operation leader, told me that the campaign had come to the Assamese as a blessing, because more than any other part of India Assam had a very large number of its population addicted to opium in a variety of ways. The campaign, Mr Phookan said, had brought about a wholesale reform and thousands had vowed never to touch opium. I should have thought that the severe condemnation that I have repeatedly expressed of the liquor policy of the Government would include condemnation of the whole of its policy regarding intoxicating drink and drugs, and that no separate condemnation was needed regarding opium, *ganja* etc. If there was no ruinous and growing expenditure on an army, kept not for the sake of preventing encroachments from without, but for suppressing Indian discontent due to the exploitation of India for the sake of Great Britain, there would be no revenue needed from immoral sources. In saying that India (meaning the Government of India) has handled the opium question with perfect honesty of purpose, Mr Campbell evidently forgets that, in the interest of revenue, opium was imposed upon China by force of arms.

Young India, 20-3-'24

80

WAR AGAINST OPIUM

The White Cross may rely upon India's co-operation in its noble work. The A.I.C.C. has only recently unanimously passed a resolution which places on record its emphatic condemnation of the opium policy of the Government of India. If every poppy plant were rooted out there would be no protest in the land against the act. The people will certainly rejoice when the whole of the revenue from intoxicating drinks and drugs is stopped and their sale absolutely prohibited except strictly as medicines to be sold by certificated chemists or druggists.

But unfortunately for us and the world, India's opinion is today represented by a Government that does not represent its people. At the forthcoming convention therefore it will not be the people of India but the foreign rule over India that will be represented, in the interests not so much of humanity as chiefly of its revenue. Whether it would serve any useful purpose to send an unofficial representative, such as Mr Andrews, truly representing the people, is a matter to be considered by the A.I.C.C.

Let us, however, see what the goal of the humanitarian crusade is. Miss La Motte has shown by unchallengeable figures that the world's production of opium is far in excess of its medical requirements and that so long as it continues, so long will the immoral and soul-destroying traffic in it continue in spite of efforts to the contrary. She has shown too that the Government of India is the greatest culprit in the matter. The goal cannot be reached till the Government of India honestly carries out the wish of the best minds of the world, immediately to reduce the cultivation of opium in its jurisdiction to the lowest term possible and without counting the cost. The Government of India alone has blocked the way and it is feared that it will do so again. And it will do so not because India wishes but because she is helpless.

Young India, 24-7-'24

81

OPIUM IN ASSAM

The Opium Inquiry Committee appointed by the Assam P.C.C. has already commenced work and examined several witnesses at Sibsagar. Many witnesses were leading men of the district and chosen from all parties. They unanimously advocated total prohibition. An experienced witness said that it was 'a preposterous suggestion that opium has any prophylactic action against Kala Azar or Malaria.' The largest number of deaths, the witness added, were among opium-eaters at Angera Khowa, a village in Sibsagar. Some witnesses gave the interesting information that temperance workers were harassed and prosecuted for 'the offence of asking people not to smoke or eat opium.' I hope that the Committee will not be satisfied with general statements but will collect comparative statistics about opium cultivation, opium shops, opium dens. There should also be medical evidence as to the effect of opium on the population of Assam. There should be evidence showing the effect likely to be produced by complete prohibition of opium. The report to be of use must be a veritable mine of information.

Young India, 24-7-'24

DRUGS, DRINK AND THE DEVIL

Drugs and drink are the two arms of the devil with which he strikes his helpless slaves into stupefaction and intoxication. And according to an illuminating article in *The Survey* on the two Opium Conferences at Geneva, opium, the chief among the drugs, 'won'. The writer says: "Out of all the marching and countermarching, the drawing of swords and putting them up again, the rumours of defeats and famous victories, the traffic in opium and other narcotic drugs has gained a new lease of life." In the midst of confusion and chaos caused by the bewildering reports on behalf of the different nations, the writer says: "The only people concerned who knew precisely what they wanted and did not want, and who were quite clear about and content with what they got, were those who in one way or another make profit out of the traffic in narcotics." "Especially during the world war," the writer adds, "the campaign has been going almost by default. In that five years of turmoil, so far as international interest or action was concerned the war against narcotics took its place with the war against Original Sin....Indeed, the war itself materially aggravated the evil. The widespread use of morphine and cocaine in the armies as anodynes against human agony, and to some extent as a means of mental relief from the deadly despairs and fears, disgusts and monotonies of war, turned loose at the end in many countries a considerable army of uncured and more or less incurable addicts to continue and spread their addiction. For, one of the awful concomitants of this vice is a kind of perverted missionary impulse to propagate itself by making new addicts."

This is one of the most deadly by-products of the late war. If it has destroyed millions of lives, it has also hastened the soul-deadening process. But Mr Gavit, the writer, shows that during the thirteen years since the International agreement was registered in the Hague Convention "the character of the problem has changed greatly." Mr Gavit can only speak from the European standpoint. Therefore, he says, "the evil is no longer an exotic affair of the Far East, of the eating, drinking and smoking of the raw and prepared opium after the time-entrenched fashions of India, China and other Oriental regions." It has now resolved itself into the use " of the more concentrated and far more injurious forms in the *high power drugs*, manufactured in the expensively equipped and scientifically-operated pharmaceutical laboratories of the lands which call themselves 'civilized'. Whereas in former times the opium and the opium-habits of the Far East were creeping out into the West, now the flow is the other way. And that is not all: these drugs are equally deadly, and spreading ominously in the countries where they are made, and across their borders to their neighbours....The threat is against the welfare of all mankind. To this devil a white addict is as useful as a black or yellow;...His is a domain upon which the sun never sets."

The writer then touches 'the heart of the evil' which is in 'the *excess of production*' beyond the very legitimate needs of medicine and science. "These needs *per capita* are:

Raw opium, 450 milligrams (about 7 grains).

Cocaine, 7 milligrams (about .11 of a grain).

This works out for a population of 744,000,000 (out of the world's assumed total of 1,747,000,000) as accessible to Western-trained medical service, to a total "medical and scientific" need *in tons* about as follows:

For medicinal opium	100 tons
„ morphine	136 „
„ codein	84 „
„ heroin	15 „
Total world need	335 „

...Of cocaine, at the rate mentioned, the requirements would be a little over 12 tons. But the total output at the very lowest is 8,600 tons. Of cocaine there are no ascertainable figures but it is nowhere under 100 tons. Thus the world's production of narcotics is more than ten times the most extravagant estimate of the world's legitimate needs."

The writer shows that none of the great powers including America and Great Britain has seriously tackled the problem. He charges them with having broken the promise made under Article 9, of the Hague Convention — "to limit the manufacture of these substances to the *bona fide* needs of medicine and science." He deplores that these civilized nations have failed not merely to check the overproduction of raw and prepared opium, but also to check even the manufacture of the deadly drugs in the huge laboratories which are subject to licence and inspection, and whose control is the easiest thing possible if there is only the will.

The readers who have studied the Assam Opium report prepared at the instance of the Congress by Mr Andrews' labours know the evil wrought by the opium-habit. They also know how the Government has failed egregiously to deal with the growing evil and how they have thwarted the efforts of reformers who tried to deal with it. It therefore did one's soul good to find that during the National Week speakers at public meetings insisted upon the total prohibition of intoxicating drinks and drugs. It is a reform that is overdue. And, if it is at all worth going to the Councils, this total prohibition must be made a prominent plank in the electoral campaign. Every member must be pledged not merely to support but to initiate and pursue the total prohibition campaign, the only way to bring about total prohibition, being to cut out from the military expenditure a portion equivalent to the revenue derived from this immoral source. The demand therefore for total prohibition must go hand in hand with the demand for reduction in the military expenditure. Nor must the solution be delayed by plans of taking referendums. In India there can be no reason for any referendum because drink and drug-habit are universally recognized as a vice.

Young India, 22-4-'26

83

OPIUM ADDICTS

A correspondent writes as follows:

"I do not know whether you are aware that in Rajputana (Marwad) the inhabitants are terrible opium addicts. A wedding or death or any ceremonial occasion necessitates the offering of opium to the visitors. It may even mean the pawning of goods or mortgaging of property, but the opium has to be offered. It is quite an ordinary matter for a person to take 1½ or 2 tolas of opium per day and sometimes even more. I know of some who can swallow as much as five. When my father died I went home. A Brahman friend came to condole. The first thing was to offer him opium which is generally kept in a special box. There were three tolas in it. The Brahman said he would help himself. To my astonishment he emptied the entire contents on the palm of his hand and swallowed them. Having done so he said he was not satisfied. When I asked him how much was sufficient he replied 'four tolas'! And of course, if opium-eaters do not get their dope at the proper time, they are no better than useless lumps of flesh. This drug habit is eating as a canker into our society."

Deenabandhu Andrews and Pearson laboured on behalf of these addicts. We have not cared for them half as much as we have for the drink addicts. The effects of opium are not so patent as of drink so far as society is concerned. But both the vices have nothing between them to choose. Slaves of opium have their reason atrophied. They become living automata, having no interest in anything but their opium. How to deal with them is a tremendous question. Not until we have an unlimited band of workers, well-trained and seasoned, will it be possible to produce an effect on these helpless members of society. The medical profession can render valuable assistance by carrying on researches and discovering remedies for dealing with this social disease.

Segaon, 4-5-'42

Harijan, 10-5-'42

DRINK, DRUGS AND GAMBLING

DRUGS

Part II : *By Others*

THE OPIUM TRAFFIC

(*By C. F. Andrews*)

As an example of what is actually happening under British rule, Miss La Motte points out, from Government statistics, that in budgeting for a revenue of 19 million dollars, the Straits Settlement derive 9 million dollars, (or nearly half their whole revenue) from *opium manufactured and exported by the British Government in India.*

In Hongkong, another British possession, and one of the most wealthy mercantile ports in the world, one-third of the whole revenue of the Colony is derived from opium, *which is also manufactured and exported by the British Government in India under a five-yearly contract.*

Further facts, disclosed in Miss La Motte's book (which are taken from Blue Books and Government Records) show beyond any doubt that, while the 'front door' into China for the Indian Opium Traffic has been closed, every 'back-door' is being used to flood China once more with opium, — only by new and underhand methods and at a much greater profit. The hateful and miserable thing is this, that the British Government in India, all through the war and since the war, has been a party to this new process of opium-poisoning China. I have with me a letter from the International Anti-Opium Association at Peking, in which the Secretary asserts, from intimate knowledge of the facts, that the greatest hindrance to the suppression of opium in China *is the production and sale of such large amounts of opium by the Indian Government.*

Take a few salient facts. Hongkong, with a small population of 500,000, has received year by year enough opium to satisfy the medical needs of 150,000,000 people. Where does most of this go to ? It is smuggled into China. Macao, with a population of about 80,000 people, has obtained opium in even greater proportional quantities. This also is used for smuggling purposes. The British Indian Government has recently signed a contract with the British Hongkong Government for another five years to supply opium, in large monthly quantities. This was acknowledged in the House of Commons. The Hongkong Government does not deny that wholesale smuggling has been going on; and yet it accepts this new opium contract, which is far in excess of its own medical needs. Why? Because its revenue depends upon this Opium Monopoly as one of its main pillars of support. The wealthy British merchants of Hongkong (who could stop the traffic tomorrow, if they tried) prefer to tax themselves lightly and to make up their revenue from opium, rather than tax themselves to the extent of the requirements of the Island. The Island of Singapore, as we have seen, has an even blacker record. The European Quarter at Shanghai bears a character in this matter, which is equally disgraceful.

With regard to Singapore, I will give Miss La Motte's experiences in her own words:

> "We learned," she writes, "that the Opium Trade was freely indulged in at Singapore, fostered by Government. Singapore is a large city of about 300,000 inhabitants, a great number of whom are Chinese. It has wide beautiful streets, magnificent quays and docks, — a splendid European city at the outposts of the Orient. We found that a large part of its revenue is derived from the Opium Traffic, — from the sale of opium and from the licence fees derived from shops where opium may be purchased, or from the divans where it may be smoked. The customers are mainly Chinese.
>
> "I wanted to visit these Government-licensed opium shops and opium dens. A friend lent me two servants as guides. We three got into rickshaws and went down to the Chinese quarter, where there are several hundreds of these places, all doing a flourishing business. It was early in the afternoon but even then trade was brisk. The people purchased their opium on entering. Each packet bears a red label, "Monopoly Opium".
>
> "In one den there was an old man, — but you can't tell whether a drug addict is old or not; he looked as they all do, grey and emaciated. As he caught my eye, he laid down the needle on which he was about to cook his opium pill, and glanced away.
>
> "Why doesn't he go on?" I asked my guide.
>
> "He is ashamed to have you see him," he replied.
>
> "But *why* should he be ashamed?" I asked. "The British Government is not ashamed to sell opium to him. Why should *he* be ashamed?"

"Nevertheless, he is ashamed," replied the guide. "You see what he looks like — what he has become. He is not quite so far gone as the others. He still feels his degradation. Most of them do not feel that way, — after a while."

"So we went on down the street. There was a dreadful monotony about it. House after house, of feeble, emaciated wrecks, all smoking Monopoly Opium; all contributing by their shame and degradation to the revenue of the mighty British Empire.

"That evening I sat on the wide verandah of the hotel, looking over a copy of the *Straits Times*. One paragraph, a despatch from London, caught my eye. 'Chinese in Liverpool. Reuter's Telegram, London, Jan. 17, 1917. Thirty-one Chinese were arrested last night during police raids on opium dens in Liverpool.'

"Coming fresh from the opium dens in Singapore, I must say that this item caused me some mental confusion. It must also be very perplexing to the Chinese. To come from a part of the British Empire, where opium smoking is freely encouraged, to Great Britain itself, where such practices are not tolerated, — the Chinese must ask themselves, why it is that the White Race is so sedulously protected, while the subject races are so eagerly encouraged. It may occur to him, that the White Race is regarded as valuable and must be preserved, and that subject races are not worth protecting."

I will quote one more passage from Miss La Motte's book, which has a terrible interest for us in India. Mauritius is a small island, which has been filled up to its fullest capacity with Indians who have gone out there under indenture. This Indian indentured system of labour, as we all know, has had an altogether pernicious moral effect, wherever it has been in force, and the degradation of Indians in Mauritius, owing to indenture, had already taken place. But now, we have from Miss La Motte the following added facts:

"The population of Mauritius is about 377,000, of which number 258,000 are Indians and 3,000 Chinese.... *The Statistics for British India*, Eighth Issue, gives these figures:

Opium exported to Mauritius from India

1912-13	..	..	..	10 Chests
1913-14	..	..	..	19 ,,
1914-15	..	..	..	23 ,,
1915-16	..	..	..	65 ,,
1916-17	..	..	..	120 ,, "

Thus, in addition to sending out these Indians, as cheap labour, under the degrading conditions of indenture, the British Government in India are still further demoralizing them by sending out this opium poison in ever increasing quantities ! This is all done to obtain revenue which is used to support the military establishment in India !

Miss La Motte gives a further quotation from the *Statistics of British India* about India itself which runs as follows :

> "During the ten years, ending 1916-17, the receipts from opium, consumed in India, increased at the rate of 44 per cent....The revenue from drugs consumed in India (excluding opium) has risen, in ten years, by 67 per cent."

Miss La Motte's comment on this statement represents the only outburst of passionate indignation in a singularly dispassionate book. She says with flaming passion :

> "A nation that can subjugate 300,000,000 helpless Indian people, and then turn them into drug addicts, for the sake of revenue, is a nation, which commits a cold-blooded atrocity unparalleled by any atrocity committed in the rage and heat of war."

Young India, 18-5-'21

85

MEMORANDUM ON OPIUM

(*By C. F. Andrews*)

[Written for the information of the members of the Council of State and the Legislative Assembly at Delhi.]

At the present time, India stands to lose the friendship of those nations of the world who are on the side of humanity in the great struggle against the opium poison, if she is unwilling to fall into line with the world reform movement, which aims at restricting the actual cultivation of opium to the full medicinal requirements of the world's population, and to leave nothing over for smuggling purposes.

This was the great issue at Geneva ; and America, China and Japan were on the side of the world reform movement. Many of the smaller nations sympathized with them. But Great Britain and the Government of India stood out stubbornly against this world solution based on restriction of *cultivation*. They suggested instead a very long process of gradual reduction of opium smoking and a stricter safeguarding of the manufactured drugs of morphia and heroin, so that they should not come into the hands of unlicensed dealers. Those powers which were financially interested in the sale and manufacture of opium into morphine and heroin sided with them.

The contention of the opium reformers was, that it is quite impossible to stop the secret sales of the drugs, when once they have been manufactured. On the other hand, it is easy to detect how much of the opium poppy, with its white flower, is being grown. 'Stop excessive cultivation,' say the reformers, 'and you get at the root of all the mischief; but once let the tiny pills of opium and its alkaloids loose upon the world and they will be sure to be consumed by someone; they will be smuggled through, and no one will be able to detect them.'

When the solution put forward by the opium reformers was rejected by the Governments of India and Great Britain, President Coolidge recalled the American delegates; and the Chinese delegates also left the Conference with them after three months of incessant delay and obstruction. Such a deadlock has been an event of world importance. It is likely to prevent America finally from becoming a member of the League of Nations. For America is saying: "If we cannot agree upon a purely humanitarian issue, such as opium, how shall we agree about political questions?"

There were two main disputes over which the break and deadlock came. In both of these unfortunately India was involved. They were as follows:

(i) With regard to India's internal consumption of opium.

(ii) With regard to India's external opium traffic.

We may take these two disputes in order and deal with them separately. Below will be found the argument in each case:

(i) Internal Consumption

The Government of India declared at Geneva that India's internal consumption of opium could not be limited to India's medicinal needs. But the opium reformers, including America, would have been satisfied, if India had agreed to reduce internal consumption approximately to the index figure of the League of Nations, which stands at 6 seers per 10,000 of population. That amount of 6 seers per 10,000 is arrived at after much calculation, and is regarded as sufficient to supply amply the full medicinal requirements to civilized people. Today, the opium figure for the whole of India is nearly 12 seers per 10,000 of the Indian population, or nearly double the estimate of the League of Nations. But while there are 'opium' addicted areas in India, where the consumption is enormously too high, there are also many whole provinces, wherein the League of Nations index figure is hardly at all exceeded. For instance, the United Provinces stands lowest, with a rate of 6 per 10,000—exactly the League of Nations figure. Bengal, Bihar and Madras stand next, with a ratio of 8 per 10,000. The Punjab stands in the middle, with an average of 11 per 10,000. Bombay is double the amount, with 22 per 10,000; and Burma's figure is 28. Assam is far the worst of all, with the alarming rate of 52 per 10,000. In some districts of Assam, where the Assamese race predominates, the rate goes up to 173 seers per 10,000 and 189 seers and even to 237 seers in one instance. The last named figure is the worst in India and Burma. In Burma, the presence of the Chinese make for a high average. We have Mergui, with its tin mines which employ Chinese labourers, with a consumption of 147 seers per 10,000 and Tavoy with 66 per 10,000 and Katha with 55 and so on. These high figures in Burma are due to the presence of Chinese who are opium smokers.

But the most alarming figures of all are probably to be found in the modern industrial centres of India itself. There the excessive consumption of opium is very marked, and we know from the records of Bombay and Ahmedabad and Calcutta how much of this is given by mothers to young babies. The figures are as follows :

Calcutta	consumes	144	seers	per	10,000
Rangoon	„	108	„	„	10,000
Ferozepore	„	60	„	„	10,000
Ludhiana	„	49	„	„	10,000
Lahore	„	40	„	„	10,000
Amritsar	„	28	„	„	10,000
Cawnpore	„	29	„	„	10,000
Ahmedabad	„	42	„	„	10,000
Bombay	„	43	„	„	10,000
Broach	„	51	„	„	10,000
Sholapur	„	35	„	„	10,000
Karachi	„	46	„	„	10,000
Hyderabad (Sind)	„	52	„	„	10,000
Madras	„	26	„	„	10,000
Cuttack	„	25	„	„	10,000
Balasore	„	56	„	„	10,000

In Calcutta and Rangoon, the presence of Chinese probably accounts for the extraordinarily high percentage. It is not difficult to see that, on the whole, the mass of the Indian village population remains remarkably free from excess in opium consumption (except in Assam and Burma). But the town population where the religious sanctions of the village life have broken down, has begun to succumb to the insidious opium habit and the danger is very great indeed of still further increase of the vicious consumption of opium. I have already mentioned the daily doping of babies. This leads to chronic constipation and children who are thus habitually doped suffer from debility and intestinal weakness for the rest of their lives. We are in danger of producing a weakly and debilitated industrial population which will be a terrible drag on the prosperity of India in the future.

Let me before passing on, give in a table the opium consumption of the different provinces and areas :

United Provinces	..	6.6 per 10,000
Bengal	..	8.1 „ 10,000
Behar & Orissa	..	8.3 „ 10,000
Madras	..	8.5 „ 10,000
N.-W. Frontier	..	10.2 „ 10,000
Punjab	..	12.0 „ 10,000
Central Provinces	..	16.1 „ 10,000
Bombay	..	22.2 „ 10,000
Burma	..	28.7 „ 10,000
Assam	..	52.1 „ 10,000
Baluchistan	..	6.0 „ 10,000
Ajmere	..	52.7 „ 10,000
Coorg	..	2.3 „ 10,000
Delhi	..	not given
Average	..	12.0 per 10,000

After examining these figures very carefully it will be seen that it is in the most thickly populated *agricultural* provinces, on the whole, that the lowest records are made. The first four provinces, whose records are fairly near the League of Nations index figure of 6 per 10,000 have a population of 170,000,000. It is clear, therefore, that if we were to deal thoroughly and drastically with what might be called the darker areas such as Assam and the industrial centres, we should effect two objects :

(a) We should counteract the terribly near danger of the vast bulk of the Indian population becoming infected — a fate which has already happened to China.

(b) We should be able to bring down the final grand total for the whole of India, which is now just double the League of Nations index figure, to a much more decent level. Indeed we might bring the All-India record within the medicinal limits recognized by the League of Nations itself.

It may be stated, without hesitation, that if we could bring the All-India figure down to 8 instead of 12, the League of Nations at Geneva would be satisfied. The actual figure for America today is 8 grains per head of the population, which works out at about 4 seers per 10,000 of the population. But Switzerland even with a Dangerous Drugs Act is as high as India's present rate of 12 seers. I have quoted these figures to show that there is still an undoubtedly large variation even in the West, where opium can only be obtained under medical prescription.

What follows from this analysis is the fact that if we seriously tackle the three outstanding evils of the present internal opium situation in India, namely,

(a) The Chinese evil in Burma and Calcutta,

(b) The Assamese race addiction,

(c) The increasing evil at industrial centres,

we might actually be able, *without a Dangerous Drugs Act at all* (which would be very difficult to work in India), to bring our opium consumption down to a much lower figure than at present and we should be able to stand a very fair comparison with Japan and the nations of the West. But for such a drastic revision and enquiry to be effective an All-India Committee must be appointed. It would not be satisfactory merely to rely on local enquiry ; for as will be seen from the above analysis, the problem must be tackled as a whole.

It ought to be made clear to everyone that Japan and the United States and practically every western country have refused to make revenue out of opium because they are aware that consumption beyond medical requirements *is a dead loss in health and strength and moral stamina to the whole nation.* As Ruskin so well pointed out, the ultimate wealth of any country is the weal, or well-being, of the people. No financial return can make up for loss of health and moral stamina. Therefore, every rupee saved from the opium revenue is equal to many rupees saved in public health and public efficiency.

(ii) External Consumption

It is now necessary to turn to the export of opium from India to the countries of the Far East for purposes of opium smoking. In the end, at Geneva, it was over this opium exported for smoking, — rather than over the internal consumption of opium in India beyond medical requirements, —that America finally broke away and left the Conference.

America publicly accused the Indian Government of conniving at a breach of a solemn contract signed and sealed at the Hague Convention of 1912-13. In the plainest possible terms and in quite undiplomatic language, Great Britain and India were accused, before the League of Nations, of a breach of treaty. Many apologetic words were uttered afterwards by Lord Robert Cecil, in trying to smooth matters over ; but in spite of all attempts at a compromise and appeals to the American delegation to withdraw the words uttered, the strong, blunt and almost brutal accusation still remained unrepealed and uncorrected.

Let us examine very carefully the actual point at which this breach occurred and the accusation which was levelled against Great Britain and India as responsible and civilized nations.

The Hague Convention of 1912-13 in Article VII states as follows :

" The contracting Powers shall prohibit the import and export of prepared opium. Those Powers, however, which are not yet ready to prohibit immediately the export of prepared opium shall prohibit it as soon as possible."

A very large proportion of the opium exported from India goes to the British possessions in the Far East. It is at once prepared by the Governments of those British possessions for opium smoking and sold in opium dens under a Government monopoly. The Government of India gets out of its contract by saying that it does not send out 'prepared' opium but 'raw' opium. The American Delegation stated that this was a mere quibble. It was a connivance between two parties at a breach of treaty and contract, because it was well known that all the opium sent out from India to the Far East was used for smoking purposes.

The British possessions in the Far East which *imported* this Indian opium took shelter under the words "shall prohibit it as soon as possible". They said that they needed time to bring the traffic to an end. The American delegates pointed out that thirteen years had already elapsed since the signing of the Hague Convention, on January 23, 1912. How much *more* time did the contracting Powers want ? Could they go on delaying till Doomsday ?

Then Lord Robert Cecil brought forward on behalf of Great Britain and India the proposal that first of all it should be ascertained by an international commission that no opium was being smuggled from China. *After that date,* fifteen years should be allowed to elapse, at the end of which the contracting Powers should agree to suppress opium smoking.

America replied that this would mean only another interminable delay. By such a dilatory course opium smoking would be suppressed somewhere near 1950. Even then, just as there had been thirteen years delay already since the signing of the Hague Convention, so there might be again still further postponement.

Then America made a last offer. America agreed to a period of 15 years delay from the present actual date, or 28 years delay from the actual date of the signing of the Hague Convention. Was not that long enough ?

Great Britain and India refused and Lord Robert Cecil insisted on his own formula of " fifteen years after it has been ascertained by an international commission that no smuggling is taking place from China." From that point, the deadlock was final.

Having signed this Article VII, we in India ought as soon as possible to have reduced our export of opium to the Far East to such amounts as are sanctioned by the League of Nations, i.e. to about 6 to 8 seers per 10,000 of population. At present, the consumption of Indian opium for smoking in the Straits Settlements, is well over 1,000 seers per 10,000 of population. The same is almost equally true of Indo-China and Macao and other Far-Eastern possessions.

Young India, 23-4-'25

86

AT GRIPS WITH THE OCTOPUS

The following is part of a letter from Shri Gopinath Bardoloi, Prime Minister for Assam, in reply to an enquiry from Gandhiji as regards the anti-opium drive of the Assam Ministry :

" It is extremely gratifying for us to intimate to you that the scheme has been a complete success in every way.

The whole of the scheme contemplated operates in three different ways. Firstly, an organization of local committees and volunteers in different centres whose main object is (1) to carry on propaganda, (2) to bring such addicts as will not willingly come for treatment to the treatment centres, and (3) to keep an eye on addicts falling a prey again to the habit through the activities of smugglers who are so plentiful and whose activities can hardly be controlled by the Excise Department unaided by local vigilance. The second part of the scheme is organization of medical centres in the areas. We have about 50 centres in which addicts are being treated. The treatment consists mainly in recouping in the system the deficiencies that are created by the use of opium. The medicines given are mainly Lecithin and Glucose. The third part of the scheme is vigilance, and it is here that we have to exercise our best judgment. Although it is only a month and twelve days since we inaugurated this scheme, you will be pleased to hear that official reports indicate that at least 70 per cent ot the addicts have already given up opium. By your blessings and of all wellwishers of the movement we feel that in three months' time the opium habit will be completely abandoned in the area where we have taken up the work. The result has heartened all workers, and we expect that the energy which has been so amply demonstrated in the work that has been done hitherto will be exhibited in an equal degree till the end. There is, however, one grave difficulty before us, and that is relapse that might come on some of the addicts if vigilance does not continue. For that purpose we are increasing our excise staff; and if the vigilance that has been exhibited by the local volunteers and workers remain, I hope addiction to the opium habit will be completely a thing of the past.

Undoubtedly the province is fulfilling itself in this great work."

Harijan, 1-7-'39

DRINK, DRUGS AND GAMBLING

TEA, COFFEE AND TOBACCO

By Gandhiji

87

EVIL OF SMOKING

In response to the request of a Calicut professor I shall now proceed to say something about cigarette smoking and coffee and tea drinking. These are not necessities of life. There are some who manage to take ten cups of coffee a day. Is it necessary for their healthy development and for keeping them awake for the performance of their duties ? If it is necessary to take coffee or tea to keep them awake, let them not drink coffee or tea but go to sleep. We must not become slaves to these things. But the majority of the people who drink coffee or tea are slaves to them. Cigars and cigarettes, whether foreign or indigenous, must be avoided. Cigarette smoking is like an opiate and the cigars that you smoke have a touch of opium about them. They get to your nerves and you cannot leave them afterwards. How can a single student foul his mouth by converting it into a chimney ? If you give up these habits of smoking cigars and cigarettes and drinking coffee and tea you will find out for yourselves how much you are able to save. A drunkard in Tolstoy's story is hesitating to execute his design of murder so long as he has not smoked his cigar. But he puffs it, and then gets up smiling and saying, 'What a coward am I,' takes the dagger and does the deed. Tolstoy spoke from experience. He has written nothing without having had personal experience of it. And he is much more against cigars and cigarettes than against drink. But do not make the mistake that between drink and tobacco, drink is a lesser evil. No. If cigarette is Beelzebub, then drink is Satan.

Young India, 15-9-'27

UNTRUTHFUL ADVERTISEMENTS

The other day I drew attention to indecent advertising. A Calcutta correspondent now sends me cuttings from well-known newspapers of advertisements which I would call untruthful. Just now a very vigorous propaganda seems to be going on in Bengal and probably in the other provinces also in favour of drinking Indian tea. The following is the translation sent by the correspondent of an advertisement in Bengali:

> " TEA DRINKING AND YOUTHFUL LOOK
>
> Jalpaiguri, May 15.
>
> That tea helps retain youthful look and energy long is, it appears, demonstrated from the experience of Shriyut Nepal Chandra Bhattacharya. He is now forty-eight, but he looks no older than thirty-four. He maintains that this youthful look of his is due to his taking tea. He had his first cup of tea when he was fourteen. Since then he has been a regular tea drinker, and since the year before last he has been taking more or less thirty cups of tea daily. In this respect he has a peculiarity all his own. He does not take tea immediately it is prepared, nor does he sip in the whole of it, but rejects a little at the bottom. He takes from six to ten cups of it at a time."

This is a specimen of many such and reads as if it were a report from the paper's own correspondent. It advances a claim for tea drinking which has no support in human experience anywhere. On the contrary, even those who advocate tea drinking advise extreme moderation. We should be no worse off, if there was no tea drunk in India. But unfortunately tea and such other so-called harmless drinks have come to stay in our midst. My plea is for due regard for truth in advertising. It is a habit with people, especially in India, to treat the printed word in a book or a newspaper as gospel truth. There is need, therefore, for extreme caution in drawing up advertisements. Untruths such as my correspondent has drawn attention to are most dangerous. To drink thirty cups of tea per day not only does not refresh the body or the mind but weakens digestion and enervates the drinker. One or two cups of weak tea per day is about as much as the human body can accommodate, perhaps, without harm. In India the tea leaves are actually boiled so as to draw all the tannin they may contain. Any doctor would testify that tannin is bad for the stomach. The Chinese know how to drink tea. They put their leaves in a strainer and pour boiling water over the leaves which are never put in the tea pot. The water has to attain only the colour of the straw. It is pale yellow, never bordering on the red as tea made generally in India. Strong tea is poison.

***Harijan*, 24-8-'35**

89

" GANDHI CIGARETTES "!

Of all the abuses to which my name has been put, I know nothing so humiliating to me as the deliberate association of my name with cigarettes. A friend has sent me a label purporting to bear my portrait. The cigarettes are called 'Mahatma Gandhi' cigarettes. Now I have a horror of smoking as I have of wines. Smoking, I consider, to be a vice. It deadens one's conscience and is often worse than drink in that it acts imperceptibly. It is a habit which is difficult to get rid of when once it seizes hold of a person. It is an expensive vice. It fouls the breath, discolours the teeth and sometimes even causes cancer. It is an unclean habit. No man has received my permission to associate my name with cigarettes. I should feel thankful if the unknown firm were to withdraw the labels from the market or if the public would refuse to buy packets bearing such labels.

***Young India*, 12-1-'21**

90

OUR TOBACCO BILL

A correspondent who is interested in a variety of reforms asks what the nation pays for her tobacco bill. I find that we pay for unmanufactured tobacco and cigarettes 213 lakhs of rupees per year. The cost is increasing every year. The import of unmanufactured tobacco which was 1¼ million lbs. in 1923 rose to 5 million in 1927. There was a corresponding increase in the import of cigarettes. If the references I have consulted are reliable, we do not export any of our own tobacco. Therefore, the value of that considerable crop has to be added to the figures quoted above. If every smoker stopped the dirty habit, refused to make of his mouth a chimney to foul his breath, damage his teeth and dull his sense of delicate discrimination, and made a present of his savings to some national cause, he would benefit both himself and the nation.

***Young India*, 5-7-'28**

91

THE SMOKING EVIL

Q. While you have all along written very strongly in favour of prohibition you have not spoken either often enough or with equal emphasis in the matter of smoking. This evil is increasing with alarming rapidity and even children are increasingly getting addicted to it. The crores that are literally burnt by smoking could be so well utilized in wise ways in our poor land.

A. The taunt is true but not new. The reason for want of equal emphasis is to be sought in the fact that smoking has attained alarming respectability. When a vice reaches that state it becomes difficult to eradicate. This admission does not mean that we should not agitate for abatement of the nuisance. How to do so and when is the question. I am sorry to have to confess my inability to answer it.

***Harijan*, 20-10-'46**

DRINK, DRUGS AND GAMBLING

GAMBLING

By Gandhiji

THE CURSE OF BETTING

"You will earn the gratitude and thanks of thousands of wives, both European and Indian, if you can succeed in putting a stop to betting at the races. My husband was an ideal husband — until he took to betting at the races. We are now in debt, and, although he draws a good salary and does not drink alcohol, we are hard up, and I am sure this is the experience of very many wives. I have often implored him on my bended knees not to go to the races, but to no purpose. And does it not seem very hard that wives and children should suffer because their husbands cannot refrain from going to the races and losing money ?

"It is true that alcohol is ruining thousands, but betting at the races is certainly ruining tens of thousands.

"By practically robbing the public, the W. I. T. Club can afford to pay its European employees handsome salaries. If you were only in the know I am sure you would agree with me that hanky-panky tricks are carried on by the Turf Club and thus the public are cheated and robbed of a lot of money. Do, for God's sake, try and right matters. Things were certainly better when the bookmakers were allowed to take bets on the race-course.

"Sir, I am sure you are acquainted with a number of men on the new Councils, and, with their aid, I do hope you will succeed in putting a stop to betting at the races. If Government would take over and manage the totes, I am sure, things would be more fair and square. The public invariably lose, and those who win, are the owners of the horses and their trainers and jockeys ; and is it not a scandalous shame that Government should connive at it, simply because some of their big officials are keenly interested in horse-racing ?

"I had better not offer my signature to this letter as my husband is in Government service ; but I pray that you will interest yourself in what I have written and succeed in stopping betting at the races."

This letter has been travelling with me for some time. The reader will share my feelings that it is a pathetic letter. Anonymous letters are rarely valuable. But this one is certainly an exception, though the writer has chosen not to disclose her name.

I know nothing of horse-racing. I have ever looked upon it with horror for its associations. I know that many men have been ruined on the race-course.

But I must confess I have not had the courage to write anything against it. Having seen even an Aga Khan, prelates, viceroys, and those that are considered the best in the land, openly patronizing it and spending thousands upon it, I have felt it to be useless to write about it. As a journalist and reformer, my function is to call public attention to those vices about which there is likelihood of public opinion being created. Much as I disapprove of vaccination, I deem it to be waste of effort to draw public attention to the evil. I must own that I had not the courage to bring the drink traffic in the campaign of purification. It has come unsought. The people have taken it up of their own accord.

The surest sign that Non-co-operation is a movement of purification is that many abuses are being removed by the people without any guidance or preaching. And it is in such hope about betting that I have published the above letter.

I am aware that the writer would be satisfied merely with some modification. What is required is a total destruction of the pest. Betting at races is a part of the gambling mania. If only the people will non-co-operate, the evil will die a natural death. Thousands who attend the race-course, do so merely for fun. They attend either to see horses run breathlessly, or because it is the fashion, but they, nevertheless, aid and abet the ruin of many a gambler.

But betting is, I apprehend, more difficult to deal with than drinking. When vice becomes a fashion and even a virtue, it is a long process to deal with it. Betting is not only fashionable but is hardly regarded as a vice. Not so drinking. Fortunately, it is still the fashion to consider drinking a weakness, if not positively a vice. Every religion has denounced it with more or less vehemence. But betting has escaped such special attention. Let us hope, however, that the vigilant public will find a more innocent recreation than attending the race-course, and thus show its disapproval of gambling at the race-course.

Young India, **27-4-'21**

93

THE CURSE OF BETTING

Babu Bhagwandas, the learned Chancellor of the National University, Kashi, has sent me extracts from *Manusmriti* on the sin of betting. I reproduce them below :

> "The king should diligently keep gambling (*dyuta*) and betting (*samahvaya*) away from the State; for these two vices destroy the State and the sovereign themselves. (221)
>
> "Gambling and betting are indeed as daylight robbery; and the ruler should endeavour diligently to eradicate them. (222)
>
> "That wherein inanimate things are used that is *dyuta*, gambling; that wherein living things are used, that is *samahvaya*, betting. (223)
>
> "He who does these himself, or causes them to be done by others, secretly or openly, may be punished by the ruler with (punishment) up to that of death, at the ruler's discretion, like cheats and impersonators pretending to follow vocations other than their rightful ones. Or gamblers and betters (*kitawah*) may be banished from the land, like those who practise prostitution under cover of dancing and singing and acting, or those who make and sell spirituous liquors and other such cruel deceivers and spreaders of vice and followers of sinful trade. (224-228)."

Young India, 25-5-'21

94

THE EVIL OF GAMBLING

A friend has been persistently asking me to draw public attention to the species of gambling prevalent in Bombay among the so-called high class people. Whilst I have been heart and soul with the friend in deploring the evil, I have not had the courage to write about it. I felt that whatever I said would be a waste of effort, as I had no hope of following up my writing by some organized constructive effort to combat the evil. Whilst I was thus debating as to writing on the evil, I had to go to Borsad in answer to the Sardar's summons. There in Borsad the Sardar and his volunteers poured into my ears harrowing tales of the havoc that gambling was working in the villages of Gujarat. It is spreading like grass fire of a windy night. Everybody is in a hurry to be rich without working. 'Somebody will have made the correct guess as to the ruling price for the day of some commodity. Why not I?' argues the gambler and rushes to his ruin. Peace is being destroyed in the once happy homes of Gujarat.

There is no doubt that whatever one calls it, this gambling is as old as Adam, and that though the form and the name may have changed, the substance has not changed at all.

The law must be against this gambling. But it is of no avail if public opinion is not behind it. It is therefore necessary for workers to bestir themselves as they did during the plague or as they have done for the earthquake relief. They must not be satisfied till the evil is rooted out. In a way it is worse than the plague or the quake. For it destroys the soul within. A person without the soul is a burden upon the earth. No doubt war against gambling is not so simple as war against plague or earthquake distress. In the latter there is more or less co-operation from the sufferers. In the former the sufferers invite and hug their sufferings. To wean the gambler from his vice is like weaning the drunkard from the drink habit. This war against gambling is therefore an uphill task. But it must be tackled. It is bad enough in Bombay. Its inroad upon the villages is a danger signal which no lover of the country can dare ignore.

Harijan, **15-6-'35**

95

GAMBLING

Gambling on the race-course is, so far as I am aware, an importation like many other importations, from the West, and if I had my way I would withdraw the protection of the law that gambling on the race-course enjoys even to the extent it does. The Congress programme being one of self-purification, as is stated in so many words in the resolution of 1920, the Congress can have nothing to do with income derived from any vice. The Ministers, will, therefore, use the authority that they have obtained for educating public opinion in the right direction and for stopping gambling in high quarters. It is useless to hope that the unwary public will not copy the bad manners of the so-called high-placed people. I have heard it argued that horse-racing is necessary for breeding good horses. There may be truth in this. Is it not possible to have horse-racing without gambling, or is gambling also an aid to the good breeding of horses ?

Harijan, 4-9-'37

96

HORSE-RACING

Q. Horse-racing is going on in many important cities. It is alike a lure for high and low, rich and poor, and it leads to moral degradation and in some cases penury. Many princes spend lakhs of their people's money on buying race horses. What steps should our new governments take to check this evil ?

A. There is no doubt whatsoever about the evil. The good it is supposed to do is extremely doubtful. And at this time of growing distress in the country it is criminal. The new national governments can do a great deal to check the evil. But let us recognize their limitations. Being popular, i.e. people's governments, they will never be able to go far in advance of popular opinion. That is specially a function belonging to reformers. But these governments can certainly, by their own example, rob the evil of the stamp of fashion that the bureaucracy has set upon it even to the point of wasting public money on the luxury. The princes will copy the example of good manners that the national governments may set.

Harijan, 7-4-'46

97

HORSE-RACING

I have written before regarding the ruination of men and money through horse-racing but a very strongly-worded letter from a friend who says that gambling on the race-course is not a lesser evil than the drink habit, constrains me to write again on this subject. The writer further says:

> "Special trains are run for the races and are full of people who wear Gandhi caps, call themselves Congressmen and go there only to waste their money. Where does this money come from? We now have popular Ministries, but they too are silent and put up with the evil."

Although, in my opinion, gambling at races is not as great an evil as drinking of alcohol, one ought not really to draw comparisons. Less bad does not make gambling a good thing. I do not know all the intricacies of horse-racing. All I can say is that if it is within the competence of a popular Government to put an end to the evil, it should certainly do so.

Sevagram, 9-8-'46
(From *Harijanbandhu*)
Harijan, 18-8-'46

INDEX

OUR LATEST PUBLICATIONS

BY MAHATMA GANDHI

ALL MEN ARE BROTHERS

This is an Indian edition of Unesco's publication of the same title containing selections from the writings of Mahatma Gandhi in his own words. As Dr. S. Radhakrishnan says in his introduction, "It is our pride that one of the greatest figures of history lived in our generation, walked with us, spoke to us, taught us the way of civilized living."

Pages ix, 253 Price Rs. 3.00 Postage etc. 90 nP.

MY NON-VIOLENCE

[Compiled by S. K. Bandopadhaya]

This is a collection of select passages on the subject from the writings and speeches of Mahatma Gandhi. As Gandhiji says, "The religion of non-violence is not meant merely for the Rishis and saints. It is meant for the common people as well."

Pages xi, 373 Price Rs. 5.00 Postage etc. Re. 1.10

BY GURDIAL MALLIK

GANDHI AND TAGORE

This is a collection of short essays suggesting some kind of an outline of values and views, common or complementary in the life and work of Mahatma Gandhi and Gurudeva Tagore. As the author concludes the life of each of them was a sacred confluence of love, labour and light.

Pages vii, 77 Price 80 nP. Postage etc. 25 nP.

HANDBOOKS OF GANDHIAN THOUGHT

BY MAHATMA GANDHI

	Price Rs. nP.	Postage etc. Rs. nP.
Panchayat Raj	0.30	0.13
Birth-control — The Right Way and the Wrong Way	0.40	0.13
The Moral Basis of Vegetarianism	0.25	0.13
The Message of the Gita	0.25	0.13
Non-violent Way to World Peace	0.35	0.13
Woman's Role in Society	0.25	0.13
Communism and Communists	0.20	0.13
My Socialism	0.35	0.13
What Jesus Means to Me	0.35	0.13
Co-operative Farming	0.20	0.13
Bread Labour	0.25	0.13
Village Industries	0.25	0.13
Trusteeship	0.25	0.13
India's Food Problem	0.40	0.13
The New Indian States	0.25	0.13
Prohibition at any Cost	0.20	0.13
Congress and Its Future	0.40	0.15
Character and Nation Building	0.40	0.15
Discourses on the Gita	0.50	0.20
Strikes	0.30	0.13
The Task before Indian Students	0.80	0.20

LATEST PUBLICATIONS

BY SUSHILA NAYAR

Kasturba	1.50	0.31

BY GENE SHARP

Gandhi Wields the Weapon of Moral Power	5.00	1.10

BY MAHATMA GANDHI

PROHIBITION AT ANY COST

Compiled by R. K. Prabhu

" Drugs and drink are the two arms of the devil. They degrade those who are addicted to them and those who traffic in them." —Gandhiji

Pages 24 Price 20 nP. Postage etc. 13 nP.

DIET AND DIET REFORM

Gandhiji's dietetic experiments were conducted with a view to finding out the most wholesome food and the wisest way of preparing it, all the time keeping in mind the poverty of our people and their slender resources. This book brings together his writings on this subject.

First Edition, Reprint Price Rs. 2.00
Pages xii, 177 Postage etc. 81 nP.

KEY TO HEALTH

" Any one who observes the rules of health mentioned in this book will find that he has got in it a real key to unlock the gates leading him to health."

— Gandhiji

First Edition, Reprint Price 50 nP.
Pages xxiv, 83 Postage etc. 19 nP.

WHY PROHIBITION

BY BHARATAN KUMARAPPA

As the author rightly says, India seems to be drifting away from Prohibition. He feels that this drift should be stopped by all means and that the public should look upon this great social legislation with favour. This booklet presents a forceful rationale of Prohibition, successfully meeting the various objections raised against it.

First Edition, Reprint Price 50 nP.
Pages iv, 43 Postage etc. 25 nP.